SUNDAY ADELAJA

Problems your shortcut to prominence

Sunday Adelaja
PROBLEMS YOUR SHORTCUT TO PROMINENCE

©2017 Sunday Adelaja

ISBN 978-1-908040-59-6

Copyright © Golden Pen Limited

Milton Keynes, United Kingdom. All rights reserved

WWW.GOLDENPENPUBLISHING.COM

This book or parts thereof may not be reproduced in any form, stored in a retrieval system, or transmitted in any form by any means — electronic, mechanical, photocopy, recording, or otherwise — without prior written permission of the author.

Cover design by Oleksander Bondaruk

Interior design by Oleksander Bondaruk

© Sunday Adelaja, 2017,
Problems your shortcut to prominence — Milton Keynes, UK: Golden Pen Limited, 2017

All rights reserved.

CONTENTS

INTRODUCTION · 7
- What the girl really did: 8

CHAPTER 1 · THE RIGHT ATTITUDE TO PROBLEMS 11
- Shelter, safe water and health 12
- You are not Immune to Problems 13
- Have a Positive Attitude 16
- From Slavery to Prime Minister 18
- The Problems You Solve Determines Your Significance 20
- Where are the Josephs'? 22

CHAPTER 2 · BE A JOSEPH; BE A PROBLEM SOLVER 25
- Here Comes The Problem Solvers 26
- The world is in need of 'Josephs' 39

CHAPTER 3 · THE SURVIVAL MENTALITY 43
- You are not needed if you are not going to be an expert in problem resolution 44
- Develop Yourself 46
- Instinctive Living 47
- The Human Mind 49
- How Human Are you? 51
- That's not what we are built for 52
- What Are You Going to be Remembered for? 53

CHAPTER 4 · SECURE YOUR PLACE IN HISTORY 61
- He solved a problem 62
- Be on Guard! 64
- Do you resemble God? 67
- Models to Emulate 69

CHAPTER 5 · THIRD-WORLD-TO-FIRST-WORLD IN ONE GENERATION 73

- The world owes You nothing 75
- Lessons from Singapore 77
- It is better to have a low-paying job than no job at all 80
- Entrepreneurship, Innovation, and Management 82
- Globalization in Singapore 84
- Singapore Today 86
- African solutions to African Problems 88

CHAPTER 6 · BE THE GOOD NEWS 93

- "I was tired of giving in" 98
- It's Time To Solve That Problem 99
- Campaign against Apartheid 106
- Is your life good news? 107

CHAPTER 7 · FOCUS ON THE SOLUTION 111

- Have a Different Worldview 113
- How bad is Africa's electricity problem? 114
- Akon Lighting Africa 116
- Think Outside The Box 119
- Solar energy is the fastest and cheapest way to light up Africa 120
- The demand for cleaner and greener alternative power sources is gaining momentum 121
- Start From Where You Are 122

CHAPTER 8 · YOU ARE HERE TO SOLVE A PROBLEM 125

- Early Life 127
- School Years 128
- Annus Mirabilis Papers and the Miracle Year 128
- The Photoelectric Effect 129
- Brownian Motion 129
- Mass-Energy Equivalence 130
- The Nobel Prize in Physics 130

CHAPTER 9 · THE POWER OF YOUR MIND 139

- Why Some People Can and Others Can't 141
- Question Your Mind 143

- Points of Interest From the Story of David and Goliath 145
- Difference Between Winners and Losers 147
- Goliath was David's Stepping Stone to Prominence..................... 151

CHAPTER 10 · EXPAND YOUR CAPACITY TO SOLVE PROBLEMS................................ 155

- Ignore the Nay-Sayers 157
- Take Action 159
- Invest Your Time 161
- Habits of Prominent Individuals..................................... 164
- Learn from Your Failures 165
- Improve On The Existing Solution 167

CHAPTER 11 · IT'S NEVER TOO LATE!................................173

- What is your Excuse?.. 173
- Lessons From Colonel Sanders 175
- You Have to Go Through Failure to Get to Success................ 176
- …1000 times!.. 176
- You're never too old to Succeed 177
- The Past Doesn't Define Your Success 177
- Giving up is the Only Sure Way to Fail 178
- It's never too late to Start Over 178
- Don't be Afraid to Start Small...................................... 179
- Just start! Seriously!... 179
- The Woman Who Changed The World of Fashion 180
- Early Life 181
- What would you do, if the odds were stacked against you? 182
- Constantly Generate New Ideas 183
- The Birth of Chanel No. 5 Perfume................................. 184
- The Little Black Dress... 184

CHAPTER 12 · STOP EXISTING, START LIVING! 189

- Just one!... 190
- They Had Their Own Share of Challenges......................... 191
- A Combination of *Love* and *Hate* **195**
- Come Up With A Plan 197
- Start living!... 199

FINAL THOUGHTS · 203

INTRODUCTION

I know before you open to this page you saw the title of the book already. And you might be wondering if everyone can become prominent? Especially, if you can become prominent? This is a question I once asked myself also. So, you are not alone.

Surprisingly, the answer to the question above is quite simple and easy. You only have to become a problem solver. But the problem with most people is that they would rather do things the hard way.

Let me share this story with you. Many years ago in a small Zezuru village, a farmer had the misfortune of owing a large sum of money to a village moneylender. The moneylender, who was old and ugly, fancied the farmer's young beautiful daughter. So the moneylender proposed a bargain. He said he would forgo the farmer's debt if he could marry his daughter. Both the farmer and his daughter were horrified by the proposal.

So the cunning money-lender suggested that they let providence decide the matter. He told them that he would put a black pebble and a white pebble into an empty money bag. Then the girl would have to pick one pebble from the bag.

1. If she picked the black pebble, she would become his wife and her father's debt would beforgiven.

2. If she picked the white pebble she need not marry him and her father's debt would still be forgiven.
3. But if she refused to pick a pebble, her father would be thrown into jail.

They were standing on a pebble strewn path in the farmer's field.

As they talked, the moneylender bent over to pick up two pebbles. As he picked them up, the sharp-eyed damsel/girl noticed that he had picked up two black pebbles and put them into the ba-g. He then asked the girl to pick a pebble from the bag.

Now, imagine that you were standing in the field. What would you have done if you were the girl? If you had to advise her, what would you have told her? Careful analysis would produce three possibilities:

1. The girl should refuse to take a pebble.
2. The girl should show that there were two black pebbles in the bag and expose the money-lender as a cheat.
3. The girl should pick a black pebble and sacrifice herself in order to save her father from his debt and imprisonment.

Take a moment to ponder over the story.

WHAT THE GIRL REALLY DID:

Well, here is what she did… The girl put her hand into the moneybag and drew out a pebble. Without looking at it, she

INTRODUCTION

fumbled and let it fall onto the pebble-strewn path where it immediately became lost among all the other pebbles.

"Oh, how clumsy of me," she said. "But never mind, if you look into the bag for the one that is left, you will be able to tell which pebble I picked."

Since the remaining pebble is black, it must be assumed that she had picked the white one. And since the money-lender dared not admit his dishonesty, the girl changed what seemed an impossible situation into an extremely advantageous one.

My dear friend, most complex problems do have a solution. It is only that we don't attempt to think about solving these problems. Come to think of it, we are surrounded with a lot of problems and those who become prominent are the ones who think about solving these problems and go ahead to take action on it. Take a look at these examples:

David became prominent because he killed Goliath. Jesus became prominent because He came to extend God's kingdom on earth. Thomas Edison became prominent because the electric bulb can now last long hours. Bill Gates became prominent because of personal computers. Nelson Mandela became prominent because he fought injustice and apartheid.

Think of any prominent individual you know and you can point out a problem that they have committed themselves to solve.

Here comes the hard part. While most people want a problem free life, the girl in the story above didn't run away from the problem. Instead, she came up with the solution.

While most Israelites ran away from Goliath including King Saul, David ran towards the problem and solved it. While most of the technology giants before Bill Gates were making cumbersome computers, Bill Gates gave live to personal computers. The end result, they all became prominent. Thanks to the problem they solved.

This book is set out to address your attitude to problems. It is set out to give you a different world view about problems because we've been taught to believe that problems are bad. But I've come to tell you that they aren't. They are the shortcuts to your prominence.

This book is about the simple things that almost anyone can do to become a problem solver. And that's why I said earlier on that the answer is *simple* and *easy*. Everyone can become prominent. After reading this book, you will know that you have the ability to become prominent, very significant and relevant to your world if you want to.

Sunday Adelaja For The Love of God, Church, and Nation

CHAPTER 1

THE RIGHT ATTITUDE TO PROBLEMS

According to UNICEF, 22,000 children die each day due to poverty. And they "die quietly in some of the poorest villages on earth, far removed from the scrutiny and the conscience of the world."

Around 27-28 percent of all children in developing countries are estimated to be underweight or stunted. The two regions that account for the bulk of the deficit are South Asia and sub-Saharan Africa.

Based on enrollment data, about 72 million children of primary school age in the developing world were not in school in 2005; 57 percent (57%) of them were girls.

Nearly a billion people entered the 21st century unable to read a book or sign their names.

Less than one per cent of what the world spent every year on weapons was needed to put every child into school by the year 2000 and yet it did not happen.

Infectious diseases continue to blight the lives of the poor across the world. An estimated 40 million people are living with HIV/AIDS, with 3 million deaths in 2004. Every year there are 350–500 million cases of malaria, with 1 million fatalities: Africa accounts for 90 percent of malarial deaths and African children account for over 80 percent of malaria victims worldwide.

The number of children in the world is roughly 2.2 billion.

The number of children in poverty is about 1 billion (that is every second child).

SHELTER, SAFE WATER AND HEALTH

For the 1.9 billion children from the developing world, there are:

640 million without adequate shelter (1 in 3)

400 million with no access to safe water (1 in 5)

270 million with no access to health services (1 in 7)

Children out of education worldwide 121 million

All these data given, attest to the fact that our world revolves around problems. And you are not immune to problems. There are a lot of problems and everywhere you turn is one problem or the other. In fact, it has become a norm for our TV stations and various media outlets around the world to give reports on different problems in the globe. I guess a day that such is not reported will be regarded as abnormal.

This has become an understatement because this generation of ours is plagued with so many problems that some have even given up on a way out. Yet, I titled this book **'Problems — Your Shortcut to Prominence.'** It's an irony, right? Yes, it might be, but it is very true. Your shortcut to prominence in life is tied to the problem you've decided to resolve.

How do I know this? Wait, and let me show you.

YOU ARE NOT IMMUNE TO PROBLEMS

All of us individually and collectively regularly face problems in our daily lives. Some of these problems could be as little or as insignificant as what clothes to put on or what to eat. This could also be as big as how will the world find a cure to a particular disease like the recent Ebola virus outbreak in West Africa that killed about 11,325 out of the 28,652 total cases recorded by the Centers for Disease Control and Prevention? Or who will feed the 1 billion hungry children in the world?

> *Many people pray to be kept out of unexpected problems. Some people pray to be able to confront and overcome them.*
> TOBA BETA

Over the years our attitudes towards these problems have defined us as individuals, and collectively as a society. Attitudes to problems vary from person to person. Some run away from problems. Some look for problems. Some hide from problems. Some look for ways of resolving problems. Some succumb to problems. But let the truth be told, Problems are our shortcuts to prominence. As such, you have to pray to be able to confront and overcome problems instead of praying to be kept out of unexpected problems.

Without much ado, in this book permit me to present my case to you that problems indeed are your shortcuts to prominence. A careful study of the history of humanity would stand as a monumental testimony to this fact.

This will take us to the biblical story of a young man named Joseph. His father's name is Jacob, and they lived in Canaan from where his grandfather was from.

JOSEPH:
The Dreamer!

Joseph was seventeen years old (old enough to drive a car these days), and he had eleven brothers, and only had one brother younger than him. Can you imagine having eleven brothers to play with, or fight with?

Because Joseph was one of the youngest sons, his father spent more time with him, and he became very special to him. So Jacob had a special robe made for Joseph. They didn't have jackets back then, so this was a very special jacket. It was very beautiful and had every color you could imagine in it.

All of Joseph's older brothers saw this and they got very jealous. The word jealous means that Joseph's brothers disliked him because they thought his father liked him more and because he got the special coat. They got so jealous they couldn't even say a kind word to him.

One day Joseph had a dream, and he went to go tell his brothers. He said, "Guess what? Last night I had a strange dream. We were tying up bunches of grain out in the field when suddenly my bunch stood up, while all of yours gathered around and bowed to me." The brothers looked at each other in disgust, but Joseph continued. "Then I had another

The Right Attitude to Problems

dream that the sun, the moon, and eleven stars bowed down to me."

"Who do you think you are?" The brothers said. "Do you think that you are better than all of us? Do you think that we would ever bow down to you?" This made the brothers dislike Joseph even more. Little did they know that the dream was a pointer to the problems he was born to solve.

When he told his father about his dreams he said, "Those are strange dreams." But he thought carefully about what Joseph had told him.

A few days later Joseph's father asked him to check on his brothers. They were in the fields quite a distance away. So Joseph went to find them.

When the brothers saw Joseph in the distance, they made a plan to kill him. But when Reuben, Joseph's oldest brother heard this he said, "Let's not kill him; just throw him in a well out here in the field." He said this because he was secretly planning to come back and rescue Joseph when the other brothers had left.

So when Joseph came to them, they took off his beautiful robe and they threw him in an empty well. A little while later a group of people came by that were wanting to sell some things in Egypt. One of the brothers spoke up, "Why don't we sell him to these people, this way we never have to see him again, and we don't have to kill him."

The other brothers liked this idea, so they sold him to the people who were going to Egypt.

Unfortunately, Reuben had been working and hadn't seen what happened. When he returned to the well he noticed that Joseph was gone. He had been sold to an important man named Potiphar, an assistant to the Pharaoh of Egypt.

The rest of the brothers took Joseph's beautiful robe and dipped it in animal blood and took it back to their father. When the father saw this he cried, "Some animal has killed my son." And he cried for many days, so much that nobody could comfort him.

HAVE A POSITIVE ATTITUDE

Joseph had a positive attitude to every challenge that came his way and this made him to overcome all the problems that he encountered in Potiphar's house, the jail and eventually, the national problem. This is the attitude that solves problem instead of running away from problems. This is the attitude that takes responsibility to solve societal problems.

> *If you have a positive attitude and constantly strive to give your best effort, eventually you will overcome your immediate problems and find you are ready for greater challenges.*
> PAT RILEY

He had started out as a slave, but the Lord was with Joseph and He helped him do everything right. So Potiphar made him his helper and put him in charge of everything that he owned.

The problem came when Potiphar's wife lied about Joseph to her husband, so Potiphar had Joseph put into jail.

The Right Attitude to Problems

The Lord was still with Joseph in jail, and the warden put Joseph in charge of all the prisoners. He never worried because the Lord was with Joseph and helped him do everything right.

After Joseph had been in jail for some time a cupbearer and baker to Pharaoh had been sent there. One night each of them had a dream and Joseph interpreted their dreams. They told their dreams to Joseph and he told the cupbearer that he would soon be let out of jail. "Please tell Pharaoh about me, and ask him to get me out of here," Joseph said.

When the cupbearer was freed he forgot about what Joseph did. So Joseph stayed in jail for two more years. Until one day, Pharaoh had a dream, and nobody could explain it to him. The cupbearer then remembered what Joseph had done for him, and Joseph was brought to Pharaoh.

If you pay careful attention here, you will discover that the problem Joseph solved some time ago for the cupbearer has now brought him to the presence of the King.

Please don't miss out on a very important point here. Joseph already solved a problem for someone two years ago before he was recommended. Don't also miss out on the fact that when they sent for him from the palace, they did not bring him there to come and warm the chair. It was because there was a problem nobody else could solve. That was why they brought Joseph into the palace.

FROM SLAVERY TO PRIME MINISTER

The problem suggests the solution.
TOM PAYNE

"Can you understand dreams?" Pharaoh asked. "I can't, but God helps me," Joseph replied. After Pharaoh had told him his dream Joseph explained, "God is warning you. There will be seven years when nothing will grow and there won't be any food for anyone."

"What can I do?" Pharaoh asked. "God has shown you what to do. There will be seven years before the bad years that will be very good. So good that there will be extra food for everyone. So you should save a little bit of each year's harvest, that way you will have enough to get you through the bad years." Joseph said.

Problems are only opportunities with thorns on them.
HUGH MILLER

The problem then, was the dream that the king needed someone to interpret for him. The solution to this same problem became the opportunity that turned the economic prospects of the nation around.

Pharaoh believed all that Joseph told him and put him in charge of all the land of Egypt. Thanks to the problem he solved.

The Right Attitude to Problems

> *⁴¹And Pharaoh said unto Joseph, See, I have set thee over all the land of Egypt. ⁴²And Pharaoh took off his ring from his hand, and put it upon Joseph's hand, and arrayed him in vestures of fine linen, and put a gold chain about his neck; ⁴³And he made him ride in the second chariot which he had, and they cried before him, Bow the knee: and he made him ruler over all the land of Egypt. ⁴⁴And Pharaoh said unto Joseph, I am Pharaoh, and without thee shall no man lift up his hand or foot in all the land of Egypt.*
>
> GENESIS 41:41-44 (KJV)

People came from all countries to buy grain from Joseph because the whole world was in need of food. Some of those people were Joseph's brothers. When his brothers came, Joseph recognized them, but they did not know who he was. It had been over 10 years since they had seen him.

The brothers all bowed to him because he was an important person. Just as he dreamed they would at the beginning. In case you have forgotten, he once had a dream that eleven stars, the moon, and the sun bowed down to him. Nevertheless, this dream only came to reality because of the problem he solved. I know you've got quite a number of brilliant dreams, but let me reiterate it; the difference between your dream and the realization of such dreams is the problems you solved along the way. It is the challenges you face and overcome. It is the issues you will have to deal with.

Tell me, how else would Joseph have come to prominence if not through problems? If he had relied on his own might and on his own power and work alone, would he have come to prominence? If not because he has solved a problem, I don't see any how Joseph could have been so prominent.

From slavery to the prime minister in just 24 hours? Little wonder I titled this book, Problems — Your Shortcut to Prominence. Resolving problems will propel you faster than you ever imagine.

THE PROBLEMS YOU SOLVE DETERMINES YOUR SIGNIFICANCE

After a few meetings with his brothers, he could not keep it in any longer and Joseph said to his brothers, "I am Joseph! Is my father alive?" But his brothers couldn't answer him because they were afraid. Then Joseph said, "Come here. I am your brother, the one you sold! Do not worry, and do not be angry with yourselves for selling me, because God has put me here to save people from starving."

So his father, his brothers, and their families came to live in Egypt with Joseph, and they had all the food they needed.

It is the problem that you solve that determines your significance. It is the problem that you have dedicated your life to resolve that determines your prominence.

Now, I am not talking about the problems that you have in your life personally. I am not talking about your problems.

The Right Attitude to Problems

I am talking about the problem that you have decided to resolve. I am talking about problems, issues, situations and circumstances that you have decided to take head on and find answers to. I am talking about circumstances, problems, issues, and challenges that you have decided to bring solutions or answers to.

It is the problems that you find answers to that determine your prominence. It is the problem that you have dedicated your life to provide an answer to that determines your significance in life. Your significance is hidden in the answers to problems that you decide to resolve.

Show me anyone that is prominent and I'll show you the problems they've dedicated their life to resolve. You will only prosper to the degree you've been able to add value to other people's life. I challenge you, become a problem solver.

If you sell food, you are solving the hunger problem. If you sell water you are solving the problem of thirst. If you sell clothes, you are solving the problem of nakedness. If you sell or rent houses, you are solving the problem of lack of shelter. If you drive a taxi or a bus, you are solving the transportation problem. If you run a school, you are solving the ignorance problem. Whatever services you are rendering, you are solving a problem or meeting the needs of others.

WHERE ARE THE JOSEPHS'?

The world is waiting for the Josephs'. You are here for resolving problems. You are here for solutions. You are not a mistake. You are not an after-thought.

Who knows? You might be the Joseph that will resolve the hunger problem. Who knows? You might be the Joseph that will save this world from deadly diseases. Who can tell if you are the one to save our educational system?

> *Expect problems and eat them for breakfast.*
> ALFRED A. MONTAPERT

Life is governed by laws and principles and there is no way around this daunting truth. A very common example is the law of gravity, which literally means that everything that goes up will surely come down. Similarly, those that expect and look for problems to resolve can never live a life of mediocrity.

Therefore, those that look for ways of resolving problems will eventually become prominent. Those that expect problems and eat them like bread will never leave this world unnoticed. Your shortest route to prominence and a life of significance is problem resolution. It is the answers you give to the questions in your society that determines your significance.

As I close this chapter, I'll like you to brood over these thoughts. You are not here for decoration. You are not a mistake. Neither are you an afterthought. I don't care what circumstances surround your birth or growing up like the

The Right Attitude to Problems

story of Joseph you just read. You are here as a solution. You are a problem solver.

> *Every problem is a gift — without problems, we would not grow.*
> ANTHONY ROBBINS

Without the problems Joseph solved, I don't see him becoming the Prime minister. It was God's gift and seed of growth planted along his path in life.

You will definitely encounter problems every now and then, because our world revolves around problems. But only the right attitude that seeks to solve these problems will guarantee your prominence.

In the next chapter, I'll be sharing with you a good number of examples of people who have become prominent, thanks to the problems they solved. They were, and some are still the Josephs' of this generation.

NUGGETS

- I know you've got quite a number of brilliant dreams, but let me reiterate it; the difference between your dream and the realization of such dreams is the problems you solved along the way.

- It is the problem that you solve that determines your significance. It is the problem that you have dedicated your life to resolve that determines your prominence.

- Show me anyone that is prominent and I'll show you the problems they've dedicated their life to resolve.

- You will only prosper to the degree you've been able to add value to other people's life.

- You are here for resolving problems. You are here for solutions. You are not a mistake. You are not an after-thought.

- Those that expect and look for problems to resolve can never live a life of mediocrity.

- Your shortest route to prominence and a life of significance is problem resolution. It is the answers you give to the questions in your society that determines your significance.

CHAPTER 2

BE A JOSEPH; BE A PROBLEM SOLVER

Do you know anyone that is prominent around you? Or do you know anyone in your life, in the bible or in history? Show me anyone that is prominent and I will prove to you that they are problem solvers. Show me any true leader and I will show you a man that has mastered the art of problem resolution.

There is a shortcut to prominence. Some people are trying to achieve prominence through their hard work alone. Some others are trying to achieve prominence through faithfulness, by being faithful to one thing or the other that they are doing. A good number of people also pray to be great.

But I tell you this that there is actually a shortcut to prominence. And unless your hard work or faithfulness is directed to resolving problems, you might never be prominent. Unless you dedicate your life to resolving problems, we might never remember you. Unless you are skillful at finding answers, you are not ready for greatness.

The only shortcut to prominence is problems. Problem is a fast track to prominence, greatness and a life of significance. Your life will only be worth celebrating if you dedicate it to solving problems.

HERE COMES THE PROBLEM SOLVERS

A good number of the people you will be reading about in this chapter are people you already know. They are the Josephs' of their generation. They are people who have dedicated their lives to solving the daunting problems in their society.

They are not people that run away from problems. They are people with the right attitude to problems. They don't hide from problems. They are problem solvers. They are men and women of solutions. And guess what! That's the only reason why you know them or you've heard of them.

Joseph became skillful at interpreting dreams. The rest of the story you already know. Similarly, you are going to be reading about men and women who moved from rags to riches. Thanks to the problems they solved. You will be reading about men who went from nothing to become prominent in the world. You will be reading about women who have immortalized themselves, thanks to the problems they solved.

Stay tuned!

MALALA:
The Girl Who Stood Up for Education and Was Shot by the Taliban

> *I don't want to be thought of as the "girl who was shot by the Taliban" but the "girl who fought for education." This is the cause to which I want to devote my life.*
> MALALA YOUSAFZAI

As a young girl, Malala Yousafzai defied the Taliban in Pakistan and demanded that girls be allowed to receive an education. She was shot in the head by a Taliban gunman in 2012, but survived and went on to receive the Nobel Peace Prize.

Malala was born on 12 July 1997 in Mingora, a town in the Swat District of north-west Pakistan. Her father, Ziauddin Yousafzai named her after Malalai, a Pashtun heroine.

Ziauddin, who has always loved learning, ran a school in Swat adjacent to the family's home. He was known as an advocate for education in Pakistan, which has the second highest number of out of school children in the world and became an outspoken opponent of Taliban efforts to restrict education and stop girls from going to school.

> *I told myself, Malala, you have already faced death. This is your second life. Don't be afraid — if you are afraid, you can't move forward.*
> MALALA YOUSAFZAI

Malala and her father received death threats but continued to speak out for the right to education.

Malala became a global advocate for the millions of girls being denied a formal education because of social, economic, legal and political factors. In 2013, Malala and Ziauddin co-founded the Malala Fund to bring awareness to the social and economic impact of girls' education and to empower girls to raise their voices, to unlock their potential and to demand change.

Notably, the Malala Fund provides funding to the Centre for Girls' Education (CGE) in northern Nigeria to support hundreds of in- and out-of-school girls through learning clubs held in spaces supplied by the local community. In these "safe spaces" led by a local mentor, groups of girls are taught reading, writing, math, and life and livelihood skills.

> *With guns, you can kill terrorists; with education, you can kill terrorism.*
> — MALALA YOUSAFZAI

Funding also supports CGE's provision of scholarships to cover school-related expenses for girls in secondary school. The program is reducing social and economic barriers to girls' education, helping to delay marriage, and expanding the critical years in which girls can acquire social assets and skills that will serve them as adults.

Malala accepted the Nobel Peace Prize on 10 December 2014 with Indian children's rights and education advocate Kailash Satyarthi. Malala contributed her entire prize money of more than $500,000 to financing the creation of a secondary school for girls in Pakistan.

If people were silent nothing would change.
MALALA YOUSAFZAI

Bill Gates: Microsoft Co-Founder; the Man who had a vision for every household to own a Personal Computer and he is transforming the world through his foundation — Bill and Melinda Gates Foundation.

Bill Gates is a prominent American entrepreneur, investor, philanthropist with a terrific career in the development of software for personal-computers. He is the co-founder of Microsoft Corporation, one of the most recognized brands in the computer industry; nearly every computer has at least one Microsoft product installed. It's no longer news that he changed the way we use and relate to personal computers today.

Bill Gates' development of software and programs has been his contribution to the revolution of computers and computer science. Microsoft's slogan was in the world. This led him to partner with several computer companies and created simple operating system and software that would be easy for everyone in the world to use.

In my honest opinion, the greatest contribution of Bill Gates to the world is providing "broad economic opportunities" to everyone across the world using computers.

Besides that, when computers combined with the internet, it greatly increased "educational opportunities" for all learners of all ages across the world and businesses thrived more than we could ever imagine. This is also a very powerful "healthcare tool" in connecting doctors with patients, and patients with the required medical knowledge in internet.

These problems solved by the software Bill Gates produced, made not only him very rich, a lot of others are now entrepreneurs online, all because a man had a vision to make every household own a computer. More importantly, it gave him the money to solve bigger problems. It is the problem that you solve that will bring money to solve other problems. Wherever there is a problem, there is money.

Coupled with his hard work, he has achieved not only the prosperity of the company but also the title of one of the richest person on Earth. Also, while being a student, Gates got inspired by the philanthropic work of John D. Rockefeller and Andrew Carnegie.

> We are all created equal in the virtual world and we can use this equality to help address some of the sociological problems that society has yet to solve in the physical world.
> BILL GATES

Since the end of June 2008, Gates has retired from an active management at Microsoft. He is putting all his efforts into Bill and Melinda Gates Foundation, which the main objective is to support projects in education and health care.

This foundation has partnered with the Global Polio Eradication Initiative made up of 4 spearheading organizations like the World Health Organization (WHO), Rotary International, United States Centers for Disease Control

Be a Joseph; Be a Problem Solver

and Prevention (CDC), United Nations Children's Fund (UNICEF).

Together, they have successfully reduced polio's outbreak by 99% and they are on course to eradicate it completely. Currently, polio has been completely eradicated from India where just barely a few years ago they had the worst outbreak recording as much as 150,000 cases per year.

Today, CDC Global Health reports that every country of the world is now polio free save for two — Pakistan and Afghanistan. However, the fight is still on-going to annihilate this disease completely.

On January 05, 2015 Bill Gates presented an ingenious machine called Omniprocessor that turns feces into clean drinking water. This installation will help 2.5 billion people in the world suffering from a shortage of drinking water.

It was developed by Janicki engineering company that is headed by CEO Peter Janicki and funded by Bill & Melinda Gates Foundation.

Bill Gates noted that the Omniprocessor could handle waste from 100,000 people, producing up to 86,000 liters of drinking water per day and a net 250 kW of electricity.

> *If you add a little to a little and do this often enough, soon it will become great.*
> HESIOD

A lot of things may be said about Gates, they may be both positive and negative. However, one thing is clear — not to recognize his influence is impossible. Definitely, the world cannot close their eyes to these problems that he is solving.

According to the ITHACA journal, the Foundation has helped lower the number of childhood deaths from 10 million in 2000 to about 6 million today. His goal is to reduce that further to 2 million, he said. He also expressed optimism that research into diseases that ravage the poorer parts of the world — malaria, cholera, tuberculosis and others — will continue to be funded.

GEORGE WASHINGTON CARVER:
one of the greatest inventors that ever lived

He transformed the Southern American Economy by inventing over a hundred products from Peanuts alone.

George Washington Carver was a prominent African-American scientist and inventor. Carver is best known for the many uses he devised for the peanut. He died in 1943.

George Washington Carver was born into slavery in Diamond, Missouri, around 1864. Carver went on to become one of the most prominent scientists and inventors of his time, as well as a teacher at the Tuskegee Institute. Carver devised over 100 products using one major crop — the peanut — including dyes, plastics, and gasoline.

Carver's work at Tuskegee included groundbreaking research on plant biology that brought him to national prominence. Many of these early experiments focused on the development of new uses for crops such as peanuts, sweet potatoes, soybeans, and pecans. The hundreds of products he invented included plastics, paints, dyes and even a kind of gasoline. He wanted poor farmers to grow alternative crops both as a source of their own food and as a source of other products to improve their quality of life.

Be a Joseph; Be a Problem Solver

An agricultural monoculture of cotton depleted the soil, and in the early 20th century the boll weevil destroyed much of the cotton crop. More so, immediately after the slave trade was abolished, there were no slaves to work on the farm. Carver's work on peanuts was intended to provide an alternative crop and this actually revamped the economy of the southern United States.

Carver's prominence as a scientific expert made him one of the most famous African-Americans and one of the best-known African-American intellectuals of his time. President Theodore Roosevelt admired his work and sought his advice on agricultural matters in the United States.

> *When you can do the common things of life in an uncommon way, you will command the attention of the world. George Washington Carver*

Carver appeared on U.S. commemorative postal stamps in 1948 and 1998, as well as a commemorative half dollar coin minted between 1951 and 1954. Numerous schools bear his name, as do two United States military vessels.

Carver's life has come to symbolize the transformative potential of education, even for those born into the most unfortunate and difficult of circumstances. He served as an example of the importance of hard work, a positive attitude, and a good education.

Carver's epitaph reads: "He could have added fortune to fame but caring for neither, he found happiness and honor in being helpful to the world."

> *No individual has any right to come into the world and go out of it without leaving behind him distinct and legitimate reasons for having passed through it.*
> — GEORGE WASHINGTON CARVER

NELSON MANDELA (1918–2013): popularly described as a world citizen

He is the man that fought for the freedom of the black race in Southern Africa sacrificing most of his adult life in the process.

> *We must use time wisely and forever realize that the time is always ripe to do right.*
> — NELSON MANDELA

Nelson Mandela became known and respected all over the world as a symbol of the struggle against apartheid and all forms of racism; the icon and the hero of African liberation.

Mandela or Madiba, as he was affectionately known, has been called a freedom fighter, a great man, South Africa's Favorite Son, a global icon and a legend, among countless other names. He has been an activist, a political prisoner, South Africa's first democratically elected president, an international peacemaker and statesman, and a Nobel Peace Prize winner.

He is the most honored political prisoner in history; having served a prison term for 27 years from 1963 to 1990. But

Be a Joseph; Be a Problem Solver

prison bars could not prevent him from continuing to inspire his people to struggle and sacrifice for their liberation.

> *I have fought against white domination, and I have fought against black domination. I have cherished the ideal of a democratic and free society in which all persons live together in harmony and with equal opportunities. It is an ideal which I hope to live for and to achieve. But if needs be, it is an ideal for which I am prepared to die.*
> — NELSON MANDELA

In the winter of 1964, Nelson Mandela arrived on Robben Island where he would spend 18 of his 27 prison years. Confined to a small cell, the floor his bed, a bucket for a toilet, he was forced to do hard labor in a quarry. He was allowed one visitor a year for 30 minutes. He could write and receive one letter every six months. But Robben Island became the crucible which transformed him.

Through his intelligence, charm and dignified defiance, Mandela eventually bent even the most brutal prison officials to his will, assumed leadership over his jailed comrades and became the master of his own prison. He emerged from it the mature leader who would fight and win the great political battles that would create a new democratic South Africa.

Problems Your Shortcut to Prominence

> *Especially for those of us who lived in single cells, you had the time to sit down and think, and we discovered that sitting down just to think is one of the best ways of keeping yourself fresh and able, to be able to address the problems facing you, and you had the opportunity, also, of examining your past.*
> NELSON MANDELA

He has received prestigious international awards, the freedom of many cities and honorary degrees from several universities. Musicians have been inspired to compose songs and music in his honor. Major international art exhibits have been dedicated to him and some of the most prominent writers have contributed to books for him and about him. Even an atomic particle has been named after him.

Mandela is a universal symbol of freedom and reconciliation, an icon representing the triumph of the human spirit. During his lifetime he not only dedicated himself to the struggle of the African people, but with his humility, and his spirit of forgiveness, he captured hearts and inspired people all over the world.

Nelson Mandela never wavered in his devotion to democracy, equality, and learning. Despite terrible provocation, he never answered racism with racism. His life is an inspiration to all who are oppressed and deprived, and to all who are opposed to oppression and deprivation.

THOMAS EDISON (1847–1931):
Thanks to Thomas Edison, the electric bulb in your room right now can last for long hours

Inventor Thomas Edison created such great innovations as the practical incandescent electric light bulb and the phonograph. A savvy businessman, he held more than 1,000 patents for his inventions.

Thomas Edison rose from humble beginnings to work as an inventor of major technology. Setting up a lab in Menlo Park, some of the products he developed included the telegraph, phonograph, the first commercially practical incandescent electric light bulb, alkaline storage batteries and Kinetograph (a camera for motion pictures).

Edison attended public school for a total of 12 weeks. A hyperactive child, prone to distraction, he was deemed "difficult" by his teacher. His mother quickly pulled him from school and taught him at home. At age 11, he showed a voracious appetite for knowledge, reading books on a wide range of subjects. In this wide-open curriculum Edison developed a process for self-education and learning independently that would serve him throughout his life.

The *phonograph* was the first machine that could record the sound of someone's voice and play it back. In 1877, Edison recorded the first words on a piece of tin foil. He recited the nursery rhyme *"Mary Had a Little Lamb,"* and the phonograph played the words back to him. This was invented by a man whose hearing was so poor that he thought of himself as "deaf"!

Starting in 1878, Edison and the muckers worked on one of his greatest achievements. The *electric light system* was more than just the incandescent lamp, or "light bulb." Edison also designed a system of power plants that make the electrical power and the wiring that brings it to people's homes. Imagine all the things you "plug in." What would your life be like without them?

A year later, Edison built a laboratory in West Orange that was ten times larger than the one in Menlo Park. In fact, it was one of the largest laboratories in the world, almost as famous as Edison himself. Well into the night, laboratory buildings glowed with electric light while the Wizard and his "muckers" turned Edison's dreams into inventions. Once, the "chief mucker" worked for three days straight, taking only short naps. Edison earned half of his 1,093 patents in West Orange.

But Edison did more than inventing. Here Edison could think of ways to make a better phonograph, for example, build it with his muckers, have them test it and make it work, then manufacture it in the factories that surrounded his laboratory. This improved phonograph could then be sold throughout the world.

Not only did Edison improve the phonograph several times, but he also worked on X-rays, storage batteries, and the first talking doll. At West Orange, he also worked on one of his greatest ideas: *motion pictures,* or "movies." The inventions made here changed the way we live even today. He worked here until his death on October 18, 1931, at the age of 84.

By that time, everyone had heard of the "Wizard" and looked up to him. The whole world called him a genius. But he knew that having a good idea was not enough. It takes hard work to make dreams into reality. That is why Edison liked to say, ***"Genius is 1% inspiration and 99% perspiration."***

THE WORLD IS IN NEED OF 'JOSEPHS'

As a close this chapter, I'll like to repeat this quote by Nelson Mandela, in case you did not pay close attention to it at first.

> *Especially for those of us who lived in single cells, you had the time to sit down and think, and we discovered that sitting down just to think is one of the best ways of keeping yourself fresh and able, to be able to address the problems facing you, and you had the opportunity, also, of examining your past.*
> NELSON MANDELA

What a man! What an attitude to problem! What kind of man will face this kind of challenges and still be bold enough to utter words like this? Only a 'Joseph' in prison.

The prison to him was a place to keep himself fresh and get new ideas. What many will see as a problem, he saw it as a golden opportunity to reflect. No wonder, when he came out of that prison, the problem that took him to prison couldn't stand him anymore. He grew so much on the inside that he crushed the problem that took him to prison.

Dear reader, the world is in need of 'Josephs' who are not afraid of problems. The world is in desperate need of men and women who have the right attitude towards problems.

Those that were shot were shot. Those that spent most of their adult lives behind bars did. Those that dedicated their wealth and all they've worked for all through their youthful age to resolve one problem or the other did because they have an understanding of problems that most people don't.

The common feature of everyone you've just read about and a whole lot of others which space will not permit me to write about is that they all ended up in greatness. The problems they solved were the key to their prominence. None! None of them lived a life of mediocrity afterwards. The world revolves around problems and only those who take these problems head on will be singled out for greatness.

Unfortunately, we have not been taught this. We have been taught to survive. We have been taught that problems are bad. We have been told to run away from problems. But that is about to change.

NUGGETS

- Show me anyone that is prominent and I will prove to you that they are problem solvers. Show me any true leader and I will show you a man that has mastered the art of problem resolution.

- Unless your hard work or faithfulness is directed to resolving problems, you might never be prominent. Unless you dedicate your life to resolving problems, we might never remember you. Unless you are skillful at finding answers, you are not ready for greatness.

- The world is in desperate need of men and women who have the right attitude towards problems.

- The world revolves around problems and only those who take these problems head on will be singled out for greatness.

- When you can do the common things of life in an uncommon way, you will command the attention of the world.

CHAPTER 3

THE SURVIVAL MENTALITY

Imagine a world without problems. The doctor without the patient. The teacher without the students. The father without the child. The cook without a hungry man. The author without a topic to write on. Imagine a world with no hurdles or goals to achieve. Imagine a world without a single problem to solve. It's a lifeless world. It's a world where you can never find real satisfaction or happiness.

> *We are built to conquer our environment, solve problems, achieve goals, and we find no real satisfaction or happiness in life without obstacles to conquer and goals to achieve.*
> MAXWELL MALTZ

In remembering this quotation, my heart yearns for the people who have not come to understand that problems are shortcuts to prominence. My heart bleeds for people who still believe that problems are bad. Little did they know that the reason why we are here in the first instance is to solve problems.

YOU ARE NOT NEEDED IF YOU ARE NOT GOING TO BE AN EXPERT IN PROBLEM RESOLUTION

Your eyes solve a problem. Your ears solve a problem. You use your mouth to eat and drink, solving the problem of hunger and thirst. Your legs move you from one place to another. So is everything that makes up your whole body. They are solving one problem or the other. Therefore, it will only be logical to conclude that if everything in you solves a problem, then your whole being shouldn't be any different.

You are built to conquer your environment. You are specially wired to solve problems. And until you begin to solve problems, you might never find real satisfaction or happiness in life.

You are not needed if you are not going to be an expert in problem resolution because you are sent to the world in the first place to resolve problems. The only reason why we need a doctor is because of diseases. The only reason why we need a teacher is because of ignorance.

You are not here to survive. You are here to conquer. You are here to subdue. You are here to have dominion over problems and all of creation.

This is evident in the Biblical story of creation.

The Survival Mentality

> *²⁶And God said, Let us make man in our image, after our likeness: and let them have dominion over the fish of the sea, and over the fowl of the air, and over the cattle, and over all the earth, and over every creeping thing that creepeth upon the earth. ²⁷So God created man in his own image, in the image of God created he him; male and female created he them. ²⁸And God blessed them, and God said unto them, Be fruitful, and multiply, and replenish the earth, and subdue it: and have dominion over the fish of the sea, and over the fowl of the air, and over every living thing that moveth upon the earth.*
>
> GENESIS 1:26-28 (KJV)

Therefore, if corruption has eaten deep into the system, it is a problem, but we have dominion. We have the ability to solve the problem. If an earthquake occurs, it is a problem, but we can't run away from it. If diseases come from microorganisms, we have been commanded to subdue them. Though the epidemic is a problem, but we have dominion over every living thing.

You are not here to survive and escape from problems. You are here to fight injustice like Malala and Nelson Mandela did. You are here to rescue the economy of your nation like George Washington Carver. You are supposed to task your mind to find answers. You are here to find the cure and drugs to treat diseases like Alexandra Fleming who discovered Penicillin did.

If the problem has a name, you are not to run away or avoid it. Call it corruption. Call it racism. Call it terrorism.

Name it. You've got to face it! Challenge it! Solve it! Find answers! Because you have the dominion, you are superior to any problem. This is the attitude of success. This is the mindset of world changers. This is the birthplace of greatness and prominence.

This is what has always led me to think and question myself every time. I challenge myself to be a solution provider. It doesn't matter what topic. I just want to be a solution provider for every problem I find around me. That's why I have been able to write 300 books to the glory of God, and I want to write more than 1000 books addressing different topics and helping people to become experts at problem solving.

DEVELOP YOURSELF

I develop myself to become an expert and skillful in problem resolution. I push myself always in bringing answers. I challenge myself in supplying solutions to any given situation or circumstance.

Dear reader, you've got to always question your mind. You have to apply your mind and make your mind work for you. Don't just exist on the earth. Don't just walk about, live to solve problems. You've got to think and come up with ideas that solve problems.

> *It is wise to direct your anger towards problems — not people; to focus your energies on answers — not excuses.*
> WILLIAM ARTHUR WARD

This is what differentiates us from the animals. We are problems solvers. You have the ability to solve any problem facing you and that is your shortcut to prominence.

Animals are only concerned about what they will eat, drink, sleep, wake up and sometimes they mate. Then, the cycle goes on. They want to survive. But is this the essence of God's investment in us meant for?

The investment of God in you is for a greater purpose, which is problem resolution. This is God's plan and God's way of taking you from mediocrity to prominence. Embrace problems today my dear brother. Welcome problems with joy my dear sister. It is your shortcut to prominence.

INSTINCTIVE LIVING

Helen Keller (1880–1968) was an American author, political activist and campaigner for deaf and blind charities. Helen became deaf and blind as a young child and had to struggle to overcome her dual disability. However, she became the first deaf-blind person to attain a bachelor's degree and became an influential campaigner for social, political and disability issues. Her public profile helped de-stigmatize blindness and deafness, and she was seen as a powerful example of someone overcoming difficult circumstances.

This is a practical example of living beyond your own very needs and reaching out to be the solution to others. Helen Keller was deaf and blind but much more she gave hope and a reason to live to every deaf and blind individual after her. There was something in her much more than her own survival. She became a beckon of hope to the hopeless.

This is what makes us different; the ability to solve problems. What makes us different from animals is the fact that we could provide solutions. It is the fact that we could resolve issues and problems. That is what makes us to be superior.

Instincts are defined as non-learned, inherited (genetic) patterns of behavior generally ensuring the survival of a species. Common examples include spinning a web by a spider, a kangaroo rat instantly performs an automatic escape jump maneuver when it hears the sound of a striking rattlesnake, even if it has never encountered a snake before, nest building and other maternal activities, migration patterns of animals, social behavior in pack animals, insects, animal courtship behaviors including monogamous mating etc. Instinctive behavior is observed more frequently in primitive life forms while more complex mammals like humans depend mostly on learned (i.e. cerebral) behavior than instincts.

We are not supposed to be living by instinct alone. Animals are the ones that are created to live by instinct. To live by instinct means caring only for what to eat, what to drink, where to sleep and who to mate with. If that is your primary concern, then you are never ever going to be prominent. You will never be remembered. I'm sorry, but that is the raw truth.

Instincts are things that are natural demands of your flesh. Instinct is what you naturally need. Why do you want to eat? This is not because you program your mind to eat; you don't need your mind to eat. You don't need your brain to eat. So, if you are functioning and doing things that you don't need your mind for that is basic instinctive or animalistic living.

The reason why you want to eat is because you get hungry. That is instinct; you don't need your brain for this. Why do you want to dress? This is because you feel shame. This is also instinctive or elementary thinking.

Animals live instinctively, and that is because they care for themselves alone. You shouldn't be bothered about yourself alone. Solve problems. There is more to life than just being bothered about what you will eat and where you will sleep. This is not the way humans are supposed to be living.

THE HUMAN MIND

Then the question is if you are a human being, why then do you need your mind? Why did God give you brain? Is it just to occupy the skull? Why do you have the ability to think?

This is because you need your mind for challenging tasks. You need your mind to resolve complex issues. You need your brain for challenging problems, to challenge your mind, to cause your brain to work, and to cause your mind to provide solutions. You need your mind to calculate things, to think ahead and to come up with complex solutions.

Problems your shortcut to prominence

> *The lizard brain is hungry, scared, angry, and horny. The lizard brain only wants to eat and be safe. The lizard brain will fight (to the death) if it has to, but would rather run away. It likes a vendetta and has no trouble getting angry. The lizard brain cares what everyone else thinks because status in the tribe is essential to its survival. A squirrel runs around looking for nuts, hiding from foxes, listening for predators, and watching for other squirrels. The squirrel does this because that's all it can do. All the squirrel has is a lizard brain. The only correct answer to 'Why did the chicken cross the road?' is 'Because its lizard brain told it to.' Wild animals are wild because the only brain they possess is a lizard brain. The lizard brain is not merely a concept. It's real, and it's living on the top of your spine, fighting for your survival. But, of course, survival and success is not the same thing. The lizard brain is the reason you're afraid, the reason you don't do all the art you can, the reason you don't ship when you can. The lizard brain is the source of the resistance.*
>
> **SETH GODIN**

So if the only thing you are thinking about is how to provide for your wife, for your husband, and children that is instinctively living. The survival instinct is responsible for this. Animals care for their families alone. They only care for their specie. They do things that are instinctively necessary to be done for their own survival.

HOW HUMAN ARE YOU?

I hope you are beginning to discover what a tragedy it is when you are been told, at times even in most of our churches that all you need is a breakthrough. And such statements as you will get your miracle today. It is all about the survival mentality.

They are not tasking you to provide solutions to the daunting problems of your nation. They are not tasking you to think and use your mind to provide solutions to the problems of electricity, infrastructure, hunger, and poverty. They are not tasking you to proffer solutions to these problems daunting the nation and the world at large. They are not tasking you to go beyond your instinct and stimulus. They are not tasking you to forget about egocentric desires and begin to think about the larger good of humanity.

They are not telling us to do anything like that. They reduce us. They reduce our value. They reduce our essence. They reduce our significance. And they just reduce us to becoming church members alone. They only reduce us to just come to church and sit down. They only reduce us to just go to a job, get a salary and bring tithes and offering.

The ability to task our brain to work is what makes us human. We are superior to animals because of our mind. How much you apply your brain determines how human you are. To the level, you apply your brain is what determines how human you are. To the level you function out of your mind is what determines how human you are.

THAT'S NOT WHAT WE ARE BUILT FOR

Apart from instinct, Animals also live by reflexes or stimulus. To live by reflexes means responding to your feelings. So if I feel like going to church, I dress up and go. If I feel like doing good, I do it. If I feel like smiling, I smile. All these are reflexes and that's what animals do.

> *A ship in harbor is safe, but that is not what ships are built for.*
> JOHN A. SHEDD

Though we have reflexes but we are not supposed to be driven by it. Though it's less demanding to live by instincts, stimulus, and reflexes but that's not what we are built for. You are meant to solve problems and live beyond you.

The third is a stimulus. Animals live by stimulus. This means you are stimulated before you do something. When you are stimulated, you do it. And many of us are not living by our own standards or goals. We are not living by our own vision and mission. We are waiting for stimulus. We are waiting to be stimulated by something, either by punishment, reward or love.

These are the animal standards of living; Instinct, reflexes, and stimulus. For example, somebody hates you and you hate the person too; somebody loves you and you love the person back; somebody smiles at you and you smile back. All these are what animals do.

THE SURVIVAL MENTALITY

The wise respond. The foolish react. The wise think and then act. The foolish act and then regret.
UNKNOWN

If you beat a dog it reacts with a shout and runs away from you, but if you gently stroke the same dog on the head, it will wag the tails. Those are stimulus and we as humans are not supposed to live that way. You are supposed to be living a much higher life. And this higher life is a life dedicated to goals, standards, and principles directed to problem solving.

WHAT ARE YOU GOING TO BE REMEMBERED FOR?

Adam and Eve are good examples, they solved the problem of extending God's kingdom on earth and that is why they are still prominent today. And their prominence is tied to the problem they resolved. Your prominence depends on the problem you will resolve on earth.

You are going to be remembered either by the problems you solved or by the problem you started. You will be remembered either by the problem you resolved or by the problem you created.

Let's take a look at two different leaders who are remembered for two different things. While Adolf Hitler is remembered for the problems he caused, Abraham Lincoln, on the other hand, is being celebrated for the problem he solved.

> *History has remembered the kings and warriors because they destroyed; art has remembered the people because they created.*
> WILLIAM MORRIS

ADOLF HITLER (1889–1945): the leader of Nazi Germany from 1934 to 1945

> *I want war. To me, all means will be right. My motto is not "Don't, whatever you do, annoy the enemy." My motto is "Destroy him by all and any means." I am the one who will wage the war!*
> ADOLF HITLER

Adolf Hitler was the leader of Nazi Germany from 1934 to 1945. He initiated World War II and oversaw fascist policies that resulted in millions of deaths.

Born in Austria in 1889, Adolf Hitler rose to power in German politics as leader of the National Socialist German Workers Party, also known as the Nazi Party. Hitler was chancellor of Germany from 1933 to 1945, serving as a dictator for the bulk of his time in power. His policies precipitated World War II and the genocide perpetrated against Jewish communities known as the Holocaust. With defeat on the horizon, Hitler committed suicide with wife Eva Braun on April 30, 1945, in his Berlin bunker.

Adolf Hitler has become infamous as a personification of human evil. His name is inexorably linked to the Holocaust and extermination of Jews and other 'undesirables'. Over 6 million Jewish people died in various concentration and extermination camps. He is also seen as the principle cause of the Second World War in which over 70 million people died. Yet, in the midst of the Great Depression, he captivated a nation with his mixture of charm, xenophobia, and almost supernatural allure.

Hitler's political programs had brought about a world war, leaving behind a devastated and impoverished Eastern and Central Europe, including Germany. His policies inflicted human suffering on an unprecedented scale and resulted in the death of tens of millions of people, including more than 20 million in the Soviet Union and six million Jews in Europe. Hitler's defeat marked the end of Germany's dominance in European history and the defeat of fascism.

On the other hand is Abraham Lincoln.

ABRAHAM LINCOLN (1809–1865): the 16th president of the United States

Abraham Lincoln was the 16th president of the United States. He preserved the Union during the U.S. Civil War and brought about the emancipation of slaves.

As a lawyer, Abraham developed a great capacity for quick thinking and oratory. In this *House Divided* speech, Lincoln gave a prophetic utterance to the potential for slavery to divide the nation.

"A house divided against itself cannot stand. I believe this government cannot endure, permanently, half slave and half free. I do not expect the Union to be dissolved — I do not expect the house to fall — but I do expect it will cease to be

divided. It will become all one thing or all the other. Either the opponents of slavery will arrest the further spread of it, and place it where the public mind shall rest in the belief that it is in the course of ultimate extinction; or its advocates will push it forward, till it shall become lawful in all the States, old as well as new — North as well as South".

To Lincoln, slavery was fundamentally wrong.

"Whenever I hear anyone arguing for slavery, I feel a strong impulse to see it tried on him personally."

On January 1, 1863, Lincoln issued his memorable Emancipation Proclamation that declared the freedom of slaves within the Confederacy.

"... all persons held as slaves within any State or designated part of a State, the people whereof shall then be in rebellion against the United States, shall be then, thenceforward, and forever free; and the Executive Government of the United States, including the military and naval authority thereof, will recognize and maintain the freedom of such persons,..."

I'm sure you definitely want to be remembered as the one who made the world a better place. I'm certain that you prefer to be the voice for the voiceless and the feet to the crippled. Definitely, I know you wouldn't pick up this book if you are not ready to be a problem solver. I'm certain that you don't want to be a part of the problem, but the solution to the problem.

It is only the problem you resolve that determines your prominence. It is only the problem you resolve that determines your significance. You are only remembered by the problem you choose to resolve. So, what problem are you living to resolve?

> *Strive not to be a success, but rather to be of value.*
> ALBERT EINSTEIN

Leave a positive impact. Life is beyond survival. It is beyond living for personal gains. Task your mind to proffer solution. Be a beckon of hope to the hopeless. Shun the survival mentality. Be a problem solver like your Heavenly father.

In the next chapter, I'll be showing you practically how to secure your place in history and how God solves and responds to problems; and this is exactly what he also wants you to do.

Remember, you are not needed if you are not going to be an expert in problem resolution because you are sent to the world in the first place to resolve problems.

Blessings!

NUGGETS

- Imagine a world with no hurdles or goals to achieve. Imagine a world without a single problem to solve. It's a lifeless world. It's a world where you can never find real satisfaction or happiness.

- You are built to conquer your environment. You are specially wired to solve problems. And until you begin to solve problems, you might never find real satisfaction or happiness in life.

- You are not here to survive. You are here to conquer. You are here to subdue. You are here to have dominion over problems and all of creation.

- If the problem has a name, you are not to run away or avoid it.

- The investment of God in you is for a greater purpose, which is problem resolution. This is God's plan and God's way of taking you from mediocrity to prominence.

- What makes us different from animals is the fact that we could provide solutions. It is the fact that we could resolve issues and problems. That is what makes us to be superior.

- To live by instinct means caring only for what to eat, what to drink, where to sleep and who to

The Survival Mentality

mate with. If that is your primary concern, then you are never ever going to be prominent.

- The ability to task our brain to work is what makes us human.

- You are going to be remembered either by the problems you solved or by the problem you started. You will be remembered either by the problem you resolved or by the problem you created.

CHAPTER 4

SECURE YOUR PLACE IN HISTORY

By now, I believe you understand that your significance in life is tied to the problems you solve. By now, you should agree with me that the only reason why anyone needs you is because of the problems you solve for them.

I dare you to answer this question honestly, have you just been surviving and trying to make a living? Has your life been about yourself alone? Is it just me, myself and I? Do you live by your instincts alone?

If you are a friend, you are solving the problem of companionship.

If you are a father, you are solving the problem of provision.

If you are a mother, you are solving the problem of care.

If you are a teacher, you are solving the problem of ignorance.

If you are a cook, you are solving the problem of hunger.

If you are a pastor, you are solving the problem of salvation.

If you are a doctor, you are solving the problem of ill-health.

Likewise, everything in your life is solving one problem or the other. Your phone is solving the problem of communication. Your wrist watch is solving a problem, it tells you time. Your bed is also solving a problem. It helps you to relax when you are tired. Money solves the problem of transaction. If they don't solve any problem, you won't need them. Similarly, you are not needed if you are not going to solve any problem.

Note, all the things I listed above, both the inanimate and the animate; none is solving a problem for itself. It is always about others. A teacher teaches others. A doctor treats others. Your wristwatch is there for you. Your bed does not rest, so it's there for you to rest on it.

What problem have you decided to solve for others? Are you going to solve any problem at all or you will leave this world without any impact? When will you be challenged to do something of significance and prominence? Will the world be glad you came?

You will only attain prominence when you decide to be an answer, a solution and hope to the cries of many. Your greatness is measured by the problems you solve. Be a problem solver. Consciously seek out ways to solve problems. Problems, it's your shortcut to prominence.

HE SOLVED A PROBLEM

Let's take a look at this scripture together:

> *²¹And they went into Capernaum, and straightway on the sabbath day he entered into the synagogue and taught. ²²And they were astonished at his doctrine: for he taught them as one that had authority, and not as the scribes. ²³And there was in their synagogue a man with an unclean spirit, and he cried out, ²⁴Saying, Let us alone; what have we to do with thee, thou Jesus of Nazareth? art thou come to destroy us? I know thee who thou art, the Holy One of God. ²⁵And Jesus rebuked him, saying, Hold thy peace, and come out of him. ²⁶And when the unclean spirit had torn him and cried with a loud voice, he came out of him. ²⁷And they were all amazed, insomuch that they questioned among themselves, saying, What thing is this? What new doctrine is this? For with authority commandeth he even the unclean spirits, and they do obey him. ²⁸And immediately his fame spread abroad throughout all the region round about Galilee.*
>
> MARK 1:21–28 (KJV)

We are just seeing an example of relevance and prominence here. Jesus appeared there and in a day His fame spread abroad. He has been in the wilderness preparing Himself to solve problems. He has fasted for forty days, listening to God and doing all he needed to do to be a solution provider.

> *...for forty days, being tempted by the devil. And He ate nothing during those days, and when they ended, He was hungry.*
> **LUKE 4:2 (AMP)**

In Mark 1:28, His fame, His prominence spread throughout the entire region round about Galilee. His fame is till spreading up till today. And the fame of Jesus will still spread tomorrow. Glory to God!

You know why? He solved a problem. You are going to be remembered only for the problems you solved or the ones you created. Your fame and your significance will be tied to the problem you resolved.

If you solve the problem of your society or country, even if it's just one problem, that will secure your place in history. It will secure your prominence in time and in eternity. It will secure your fame because you resolve one problem.

Solving problems, conquering challenges, finding answers is what gives you a sense of living. Until you dedicate your life to problem resolution, you've not started living. Greatness will still be far-fetched until you decide to devote your wealth, time and resources to solving one problem or the other.

BE ON GUARD!

Listen my dear friend; anything that takes your focus off problem resolution is a threat to your greatness. Anything that does not allow you find solutions to problems is directly fighting your significance in life. Anything that drains your energy off solving problems reduces your value. It reduces your essence. It will limit you to a live of mediocrity. So, be on the guard. Unfortunately, religion reduces your value. Religion reduces us when it doesn't challenge us to go and resolve problems. It reduces us when it doesn't challenge us to go and resolve issues, to go and bring solutions, and answers to the daunting problems of our age. Religion reduces our significance. It's a shame!

> *Religion is the opium of the masses.*
> KARL MARX

A greater tragedy is the fact that our churches today are filled with people who are only concerned with meeting their instinctive desires alone. The people in our churches today only care about the instinctive desires of their lives. They come to church to pray for provision — what to eat. They pray for better job opportunities. They pray for miracle money and the likes.

I'm afraid that our churches don't talk about all these things. I'm afraid that our churches only talk about our instinct. They keep us at the animalistic level of living. They don't talk to us about things that really make us humans. They keep us at the level of feelings. They keep us on the level of reflexes. They keep us on the level of instincts.

> *Any religion that professes to be concerned about the souls of men and is not concerned about the slums that damn them, the economic conditions that strangle them and the social conditions that cripple them is a spiritually moribund religion awaiting burial.*
> **Martin Luther King, Jr.**

We are not told that our problems are the challenges that bring out the creativity and innovative power of God in us. We are never told to face our challenges head on. We are only told to depend on God. They say, *"God will do it."*

But what makes us to be in the likeness and image of God is the fact that we have the ability to solve problems. God started by resolving problems. He came from heaven and saw darkness, everything was dark and void. That is a problem right there. It was a challenge.

> ¹*In the beginning God created the heaven and the earth.* ²*And the earth was without form and void, and darkness was upon the face of the deep. And the Spirit of God moved upon the face of the waters.*
> **Genesis 1:1-2 (KJV)**

And what did God do? Did He just sit in heaven to enjoy His problem free life? Is that what God did? NO!

God is not so irresponsible. Our God is not an irresponsible God. My God is not an irresponsible God. He doesn't run away from problems. He runs to them. He challenges Himself to solve them.

As a responsible God, He saw it as necessary, He saw it as something that He must take upon Himself to face the challenge of His day. And the challenge of that hour was to get rid of that darkness. He took it upon Himself as a challenge to remove the darkness and to bring shape and form to the earth, which is the beautiful earth that you see today.

> *And God made two great lights; the greater light to rule the day, and the lesser light to rule the night: he made the stars also.*
> GENESIS 1:16 (KJV)

The answer God came up with is the sun and the moon that we are enjoying today. The answer did not only bring light on earth, it also brought life to plants and animals. The only way you resemble God is by solving problems.

DO YOU RESEMBLE GOD?

Don't you tell me you are in His image if you are not doing the same thing God is doing? Don't you tell me you are God's image if you are not looking for problems to solve! Don't you tell me you are created in His image if you are not doing the same thing your father did? Don't you tell me you are His image if you are not copying Him! Don't you tell me you are God's child if you are not doing what your father does. Don't you tell me you resemble Him if you are not acting like Him!

> ^{26}*And God said, Let us make man in our image, after our likeness: and let them have dominion over the fish of the sea, and over the fowl of the air, and over the cattle, and over all the earth, and over every creeping thing that creepeth upon the earth.* ^{27}*So God created man in his own image, in the image of God created he him; male and female created he them.*
> GENESIS 1:26-27 (KJV)

Do you resemble God? You are created in His image and likeness but do you resemble your maker?

God is a creator, what are you creating? What have you created? He is an answer provider, what things are you finding answers to? He is a solution giver, what things are you giving solutions to? Where is the list of the problems of your age? Where is the list of the problems in your country? Where are the lists of the problems of your time, generation? What are the problems facing your town or city? What are the problems that are challenging you? What are the problems that concern you? What are the issues that concern you?

What things are you doing to bring about answers? What things are you doing to bring about solutions to these problems? That's what God did and He's still doing today. That's why He is the answer. That's why He is the creator. And He made you and me in His image to be co-creators with Him.

Listen my dear friend; you only have one shot at life. You only have one chance to live. You will leave this world soon and you will be forgotten if you fail to be an answer to at least a problem in your time. Your shortcut to prominence is problems. Your shortcut to prominence is problems. Your shortcut to prominence is problems. To leave a lasting legacy, be an answer to a problem.

You will be forgotten and will never be remembered if you don't begin to live to find solutions and answers right now.

You must ask yourself, what area, and where do you want to bring answers to. You must become an expert in bringing solutions and answers. If you don't do that, you will die and you will be forgotten.

God is a solution provider. That's His nature and I suppose we are His children. I suppose He is our father. How do you resemble God? Tell me, how you resemble Him! Do you resemble Him in providing answers? Do you resemble Him in supplying solutions? How are you equipping yourself to be able to do that? How do you push yourself? How do you educate yourself? How do you work on yourself to be able to bring a lasting solution to a problem?

Will you be able to lift up your head and quit just living for yourself and your family? Will you be able to stop living that selfish and egocentric life?

MODELS TO EMULATE

Enoch in Genesis 5:24 resolved the problem of man walking with God. He made us understand that it is possible for human beings to discover and to walk with God on the earth by faith. That is the problem Enoch resolved for us. And thanks to him we know that it is possible for human beings to walk with God on earth today.

Abel, Cain's brother in Genesis 4 resolved the problem of serving and sacrificing to God. He showed us what it means to truly sacrifice for God.

Abraham in Genesis 17:5 started a new generation and through his example, we came to understand that a human being could start a new generation of people. By faith, Abraham believed God and inherited a distant city, a new nation that is yet to be built. One man became a blessing to the whole world. That is the problem that Abraham resolved for us.

Every human being that is prominent, everyone that you remember got there as a direct result of the problem they resolved. My dear friend, what problem are you going to resolve? What problem are you going to be prominent for? What problem are you going to be remembered for?

Sarah, Abraham's wife resolved the problem of giving birth to a child in hopelessness. She became a beckon of hope to a lot of women looking for the fruit of the womb. When all hope was gone, she believed God with her husband and brought forth a child at an old age.

In Exodus 3: 10 (AMP), God was speaking to Moses about his mission.

"Therefore, come now, and I will send you to Pharaoh, and then bring My people, the children of Israel, out of Egypt."

Moses resolved the problem of captivity. He resolved the problem of how a nation could be delivered. He showed us that a whole nation could be delivered from whatsoever bondage that may exist. He showed us that God could use one man to deliver His promise to a people. He resolved the problem to make us know that it is possible. It is possible that we all could be deliverers of nations.

Bill Gates resolved the problem of personal computers. He made it possible that every household has access to personal computers. Steve Jobs of Apple Computers resolved the problem of smart phones making communication a lot easier. Now, a good number of families around the world owns a Personal Computer or carry them around in smart phones.

My dear friend if you have to go to school, make sure you are educated to be a problem solver. If you have to go to church, make sure you are been tasked to solve problems. If you have to learn anything, learn how to solve problems. In whatever you do, be an expert in resolving problems. That is your only security for stardom. That is your shortcut to prominence.

You might just be the one to bring a solution to the problem of female child education and premarital pregnancy in your country. It may be to bring a solution to the stigmatization of barren women. It could also be the solution to religious intolerance in your country.

Whatever your burden might be, it should be set before you as a goal. Whatever you have a passion for should be your standard for living.

Come along with me to the next chapter and I will show you how a nation turned the tables in their favor by taking responsibility to solve their own problems.

NUGGETS

- Your greatness is measured by the problems you solve. Be a problem solver.

- If you solve the problem of your society or country, even if it's just one problem, that will secure your place in history.

- Solving problems, conquering challenges, finding answers is what gives you a sense of living.

- Listen my dear friend; anything that takes your focus off problem resolution is a threat to your greatness. Anything that does not allow you find solutions to problems is directly fighting your significance in life.

- The only way you resemble God is by solving problems.

- You only have one chance to live. You will leave this world soon and you will be forgotten if you fail to be an answer to at least a problem in your time.

- If you have to go to school, make sure you are educated to be a problem solver. If you have to go to church, make sure you are been tasked to solve problems. If you have to learn anything, learn how to solve problems. In whatever you do, be an expert in resolving problems.

CHAPTER 5

THIRD-WORLD-TO-FIRST-WORLD IN ONE GENERATION

So many times I have been approached to own a property or to have a house in my country Nigeria. And on several occasions, I've actually come with money thinking I will buy a house in Lagos or some other place. But each time I've turned back without buying anything. The reason been I see so many problems around me.

By the time I drive from the airport to the place where they want me to buy the house, I've seen so much sorrow, tragedy, problems that I lose appetite. So much that I lose the desire to even own a house there. I even lose the desire to do any other thing other than resolving the problems.

I don't think this is just about Nigeria. Just today I was looking into the internet and I saw the picture of one of the cities in Africa, everywhere you look is problem. And the impression you have is that nobody cares about all these problems. The impression you have is that nobody even notices all these problems.

And I just keep on thinking; don't we know this is our chance? Don't you know this is your opportunity for greatness and prominence?

For example, I saw electric poles in the street all over the City. They are electric poles with wires carrying electricity right in the city. And it just paints a very ugly picture. I mean you see the electric wires just hanging everywhere in the city creating a very ugly picture.

With a country of about 180million people, why can't anybody do something about it? Some of these people studied engineering, and not just engineering but electrical engineering. And it has not even crossed their mind to come up with an idea on how to build and clean up our cities. Remove all the wires and the pillars and just make the city and country decent.

Let's even assume we don't have an idea of how to resolve it. Many of the leaders in the country have travelled to a lot of European countries. Has it not crossed somebody's mind that when you go to Europe or America, all these ugly sights are not seen? Can't you ask questions of how it's been done in these places? At least let's just copy them.

This is one problem that does not bother anyone, despite the fact that those electric poles fall down and people get electrocuted at times during rainfalls. Still, it doesn't even come to the mind of the government or the leaders to provide a lasting solution.

Let me just share with you a story of a nation, a former British colony, but unlike Nigeria, they took responsibility for their problems and have grown from a third world nation to a first world nation in one generation. As I hope that you and I will be able to come up with African solutions to African Problems. Even though I won't advocate that we copy everything they did, but there are quite a number of lessons you can learn from it.

THE WORLD OWES YOU NOTHING

At its birth Singapore had no natural resources save for its location and its people. This staggering fact made one of her leaders to say this in an interview, "*The world owes us nothing, if we didn't get up and do something for ourselves and make ourselves relevant and useful to the world, then we will just go back to being a fishing village of a hundred and fifty souls which was what the place could support in its natural state.*"

Few gave tiny Singapore much chance of survival when it was granted independence in 1965. How is it, then, that today the former British colonial trading post is a thriving Asian metropolis with not only the world's number one airline, best airport, and busiest port of trade but also the world's fourth-highest per capita real income?

Rising from a legacy of divisive colonialism, the devastation of the Second World War, and general poverty and disorder following the withdrawal of foreign forces, Singapore now is hailed as a city of the future. This miraculous history is dramatically recounted by the man who not only lived through it all but who fearlessly forged ahead and brought about most of these changes.

Certainly, there is much to learn from Singapore's rapid transition from a malaria-ridden swamp to an innovation and technology leader. Singapore also boasts of having one of the most efficient postal, telephone, and telegraph services in Southeast Asia.

Problems Your Shortcut to Prominence

Fifty years ago, the city-state of Singapore was an undeveloped country with a GDP per capita of less than US $320. Today, it is one of the world's fastest growing economies. Its GDP per capita has risen to an incredible US $60,000, making it the sixth highest in the world based on Central Intelligence Agency figures.

For a country that lacks territory and natural resources, Singapore's economic ascension is nothing short of remarkable. By embracing globalization, free market capitalism, education, and strict pragmatic policies, the country has been able to overcome their geographic disadvantages and become a leader in global commerce.

Just before you get too carried away, it will be very necessary at this point for me to let you know that Singapore was not without problems at inception. The way they responded to these problems is the lesson I want us to learn. They solved their own problems and today, the beauty of the nation speaks for her.

Singapore gained formal independence on August 9, 1965, with Yusof bin Ishak serving as its first president and the highly influential Lee Kuan Yew as its Prime Minister.

Upon independence, Singapore continued to experience problems. Much of the city-state's three million people were unemployed. More than two-thirds of its population was living in slums and squatter settlements on the city's fringe. The territory was sandwiched between two large and unfriendly states in Malaysia and Indonesia. It lacked natural resources, sanitation, proper infrastructure, and adequate water supply. In order to stimulate development, Lee sought international assistance, but his pleas went unanswered, leaving Singapore to fend for itself.

LESSONS FROM SINGAPORE

The Singapore model that transformed this former British colonial outpost into a tidy, gleaming metropolis was a mix of semi-authoritarian, one-party rule; meticulous urban planning; laissez-faire economic policies; low taxes; and heaps of imported foreign talent. The loss of personal freedoms and government intrusiveness — like muzzling political dissent and issuing fines for failing to flush public toilets — in exchange for order and prosperity was a trade-off broadly accepted by a generation of Singaporeans who saw their country's living standards rocket beyond those of its neighbors.

Most of this significant development has been credited to the Singapore's first and longest serving Prime Minister Lee Kuan Yew, regarded as one of the most influential political figures in Asia. He transformed a colonial trading post into one of the world's most important financial centers through the "Singapore economic miracle," before his death at the age 91.

> *I have spent my life, so much of it, building up this country. There's nothing more that I need to do. At the end of the day, what have I got? A successful Singapore. What have I given up? My life.*
>
> LEE KUAN YEW

He and a small group of Singaporean leaders banded together and, by "getting the basics right," transformed a poor and polyglot city into an astonishingly successful modern nation. Lee tells in crisp and polished prose how this group identified the key problems of nation-building, analyzed what needed to be done, and then — with uncompromising determination — did it.

Singapore has overtaken Hong Kong and Japan, as well as established European economies such as the UK. Prime Minister Lee Kuan Yew's policy was aimed at encouraging savings and investment, keeping inflation and taxes low and currencies stable, and emphasizing high-quality education.

Lee Kuan Yew came to power in 1959 and led Singapore to independence from Malaysia in 1965. A tiny land with no natural resources turned into a global economic powerhouse under his guidance. *"I was trying to create, in a third world situation, a first world oasis,"* Lee said in an interview in 2008.

The economy of modern Singapore is known as one of the freest, most innovative and business-friendly, according to the Asian Century Institute. It was ranked the second freest economy in the 2011 Index of Economic Freedom behind Hong Kong. The Global Competitiveness Index 2012-2013 ranks Singapore as the most competitive country in the world.

Prime Minister Lee underlined the role of government rather than the free hand of the market. Singapore today attracts a large amount of foreign investment as a result of its corruption-free environment, low tax rates and advanced infrastructure.

Foreign direct investment in the country amounted to $534 billion in 2011; according to the 2014 Investment Climate report from Singapore's government. Singapore has a 7 percent corporate tax and 0-20 percent personal tax rate. More than 7,000 multinational corporations from the United States, Japan, and Europe are located in the country.

Singapore made sure that the best and brightest were attracted, that they were paid properly, and they were given full support by leadership to do their job. As Lee observed "equal opportunities for all and meritocracy, with the best man or woman for the job, especially in leaders in government", were "basic principles that have helped us progress".

With delegated power and authority went responsibility of course.

In contrast to the xenophobia and identity politics suffered in Africa, the importation of talent has been another key aspect. Instead, most of our best and brightest minds leave for so called better opportunities outside the continent. Little did they know that resolving these problems in their country is a shortcut to their prominence.

From little over one million people at independence, of Singapore's current population of 5.3 million, around 1.5 million are expatriates, permanent residents or migrant workers. The injection of immigrants is part of a strategy to maintain GDP targets and synchs with the need for Singapore's continuous innovation and efficiency.

IT IS BETTER TO HAVE A LOW-PAYING JOB THAN NO JOB AT ALL

A very flexible labor market helps companies to withstand external shocks, changes, and challenges, driven by a philosophy that '**it is better to have a low-paying job than no job at all**' – a political anathema in contemporary Nigeria, to take one African example. In Singapore, too, a symbiotic relationship is structured between government, the unions, and business.

All this has been underpinned by a drive to globalize rather than nationalize. Whereas African countries routinely make it difficult to move goods in and out and are inherently suspicious of the motives of foreign investors, Singapore has capitalized on its strategic geographic crossroads by matching policies and the focus of institutions — there is a zero tariff on imported goods, low tax rates, a range of free trade agreements, vigorous trade and export promotion, and nearly 40,000 international corporations on the island, including 7,000 multinationals.

Singapore has avoided trying to buck the markets or the needs and sensitivities of multinational companies and international finance. To the contrary, it has always acted to strengthen regulatory institutions to negate any perception of developing country risk.

Singapore is thus a "right lesson" for Africa in leadership, planning, continuous innovation, commercial logic and using its only natural resource — its people and minds — to best effect.

Third-World-to-First-World in One Generation

By the 1990s, Singapore's per capita GDP was higher than that of its erstwhile colonial master Britain. Today Singapore has the world's busiest port and is the third-largest oil refiner. Under Lee's leadership, it has shown what is achievable with better choices in little more than a generation.

A remarkable aspect of Singapore's transition is in its unwillingness to look back. Whereas many African nations berate colonialism at every turn (not least since it offers the prospect of aid and of externalizing their problems and excusing regime inadequacies), Singaporeans seldom mention history as an excuse.

Perhaps Lee's greatest legacy was to set Singapore in a direction looking forward. In so doing, he has left an extraordinary legacy, for his own country of course, but also for others aspiring to follow a similar development path.

His key message on the driving force behind Singapore's success is simple: *"The quality of a nation's manpower resources is the single most important factor determining national competitiveness. It is the people's innovativeness, entrepreneurship, team work, and their work ethic that gives them that sharp keen edge in competitiveness."*

He emphasizes the importance of knowledge in economic transformation but also rejects the classical separation between scholarship and entrepreneurship. *"Those with good minds to be scholars should also be inventors, innovators, venture capitalists, and entrepreneurs; they must bring new products and services to the market to enrich the lives of people everywhere."*

This lesson from the evolution of Singapore's educational system poses great challenges for most developing countries.

ENTREPRENEURSHIP, INNOVATION, AND MANAGEMENT

How to reform educational systems to keep pace with contemporary challenges is one of the most important leadership lessons that developing countries can learn from Singapore. In stating that "demography, not democracy, will be the most critical factor for security in the 21st century," Lee Kuan Yew emphasizes his belief in the supremacy of the quality of human capital.

He connects this to three attributes that he considers vital for global competitiveness: entrepreneurship (seeking out opportunities and taking calculated risks); innovation (creating new products and processes that add value); and management (opening new markets and distribution channels).

Probably the most enduring theme in Lee Kuan Yew's leadership style and conviction is the role of learning. His vision of workers of the future reflects greater autonomy "to manage their own control systems, supervise themselves, and take upon themselves the responsibility to upgrade. They must be disciplined enough to think on their own and to seek to excel without someone breathing down their neck."

This lesson might appear to run counter to popular perceptions about Lee Kuan Yew's own leadership style. But he expects the same kind of "creativity of the leadership, its willingness to learn from experience elsewhere, to implement good ideas quickly and decisively through an efficient public service."

In addition, he argues for a leadership style that can "convince the majority of people that tough reforms are worth taking, that decide a country's development and progress."

One of the critical areas that require tough decisions includes large infrastructure investments that lay the foundations for economic growth. Singapore built "world-class infrastructure…good communications by air, by sea, by cable, by satellite, and now over the Internet." But such long-term investments demand not only having a long-term economic vision but consistence and predictability in the rule of law.

Lee Kuan Yew remains optimistic about the economic future of developing countries: *"There is no reason why third world leaders cannot succeed…if they can maintain social order, educate their people, maintain peace with their neighbors, and gain the confidence of investors by upholding the rule of law."*

To achieve success, these leaders must have Lee Kuan Yew's determination, consistency, and persistence. They must set out to do something concrete and cannot just focus on the trappings of statesmanship.

For developing countries, history can repeat itself, but not necessarily in the caustically pessimistic way that Karl Marx describes when he said it repeats itself "first as tragedy, second as farce." Lee Kuan Yew presents a more optimistic outlook. His insights are an important source of inspiration for present and future leaders.

GLOBALIZATION IN SINGAPORE

During colonial times, Singapore's economy was centered on entrepôt trade. But this economic activity offered little prospect for job expansion in the post-colonial period. The withdrawal of the British further aggravated the unemployment situation.

The most feasible solution to Singapore's economic and unemployment woes was to embark on a comprehensive program of industrialization, with a focus on labor-intensive industries. Unfortunately, Singapore had no industrial tradition.

The majority of its working population was in trade and services. Therefore, they had no expertise or easily adaptable traits in the area. Moreover, without a hinterland and neighbors who would trade with it, Singapore was forced to look for opportunities well beyond its borders to spearhead its industrial development.

Pressured to find work for their people, the leaders of Singapore began to experiment with globalization. Influenced by Israel's ability to leap over its Arab neighbors who boycotted them and trade with Europe and America, Lee and his colleagues knew they had to connect with the developed world and to convince their multinational corporations to manufacture in Singapore.

In order to attract investors, Singapore had to create an environment that was safe, corruption- free, low in taxation, and unimpeded by unions. To make this feasible, the citizens of the country had to suspend a large measure of their freedom in place of a more autocratic government.

Anyone caught conducting a narcotic trade or intensive corruption would be met with the death penalty. Lee's People Action Party (PAP) repressed all independent labor unions and consolidated what remained into a single umbrella group called the National Trade Union Congress (NTUC), which it directly controlled. Individuals who threatened national, political, or corporate unity were quickly jailed without much due process.

The country's draconian, but business-friendly laws became very appealing to international investors. In contrast to their neighbors, where political and economic climates were unpredictable, Singapore on the other hand, was very predictable and stable. Moreover, with its advantageous relative location and established port system, Singapore was an ideal place to manufacture out of.

By 1972, just seven years since independence, one-quarter of Singapore's manufacturing firms were either foreign-owned or joint-venture companies, and both the U.S. and Japan were major investors. As a result of Singapore's steady climate, favorable investment conditions and the rapid expansion of the world economy from 1965 to 1972, the country's Gross Domestic Product (GDP) experienced annual double-digit growth.

As foreign investment poured in, Singapore began focusing on developing its human resources, in addition to its infrastructure. The country set up many technical schools and paid international corporations to train their unskilled workers in information technology, petrochemicals, and electronics. For those who could not get industrial jobs, the government enrolled them in labor intensive un-tradable services, such as tourism and transportation.

The strategy of having multinationals educate their workforce paid great dividends for the country. In the 1970s, Singapore was primarily exporting textiles, garments, and basic electronics. By the 1990s, they were engaging in wafer fabrication, logistics, biotech research, pharmaceuticals, integrated circuit design, and aerospace engineering.

SINGAPORE TODAY

Today, Singapore is an ultra-industrialized society and entrepôt trade continues to play a central role in its economy. The Port of Singapore is now the world's busiest transshipment port, surpassing Hong Kong and Rotterdam. In terms of total cargo tonnage handled, it has become the world's second busiest, behind only the Port of Shanghai.

Singapore's tourism industry is also thriving, attracting over 10 million visitors annually. The city-state now has a zoo, night safari, and a nature reserve. The country recently opened two of the world's most expensive integrated casino resorts in the Marina Bay Sands and the Resorts World Sentosa. The country's medical tourism and culinary tourism industries have also become quite marketable, thanks to its mosaic of cultural heritage and advance medical technology.

Banking has grown significantly in recent years and many assets formerly held in Switzerland have been moved to Singapore due to new taxes imposed by the Swiss. The biotech industry is burgeoning, with drug makers such as GlaxoSmithKline, Pfizer, and Merck & Co. all establishing plants there, and oil refining continues to play a huge role in the economy.

Despite its small size, Singapore is now the fifteenth largest trading partner of the United States. The country has established strong trade agreements with several countries in South America, Europe, and Asia, as well. There are currently over 3,000 multinational corporations operating in the country, accounting for more than two-thirds of its manufacturing output and direct export sales.

With a total land area of just 433 square miles and a small labor force of 3 million people, Singapore is able to produce a GDP that exceeds $300 billion dollars annually, higher than three-quarters of the world. Life expectancy is at an average of 83.75 years, making it the third highest globally. The corruption minimal and so is the crime. It is considered to be one of the best places to live on earth if you don't mind the strict rules.

Singapore, with a population of about 5.5million people, now boasts the third highest GDP per capita in the world and one of the world's highest life expectancies (equal second with 83). It is now one of the richest countries on the planet with an economy entirely incommensurate for its tiny size.

Bereft of any natural resources, a young Prime Minister pushed the island to develop her human capital and key infrastructure, including a world-class port and an airport. Truly, they've been able to *create, in a third world situation, a first world oasis.*

AFRICAN SOLUTIONS TO AFRICAN PROBLEMS

Who knows, you might be the President of your nation tomorrow and the problems you solve will determine the prominence of that nation. Even if you don't occupy any leadership position in government, there is so much you can do.

Remember, George Washington Carver, who had over 100 inventions from peanuts alone and this saved the Southern America economy immediately after the slave trade was abolished, was not a politician. Malala and Bill Gates also aren't, but the world is feeling their impact.

I believe this story can inspire you to innovatively solve the problems of your nation. I believe we can begin to come up with African solutions to African Problems.

I started with this quote and I will like to conclude using it again due to its importance.

"The world owes us nothing, if we didn't get up and do something for ourselves and make ourselves relevant and useful to the world, then we will just go back to being a fishing village of a hundred and fifty souls which was what the place could support in its natural state."

My dear friends, the world owes you nothing. Get up on your feet and challenge yourself to solve the problems of your nation. Complains have not and will not solve our problems. Instead, tasking our minds to innovatively and creatively solve these problems will.

As a Nigerian, as an African or as a citizen of any developing nation in the world, if you don't get up and do something for yourself and your nation, don't expect to be useful, respected or relevant to the world. Yes, You! You, reading this! Get up on your feet.

The problem you solve is your shortcut to prominence.

NUGGETS

- Singapore is a "right lesson" for Africa in leadership, planning, continuous innovation, commercial logic and using its only natural resource — its people and minds — to best effect.

- The quality of a nation's manpower resources is the single most important factor determining national competitiveness. It is the people's innovativeness, entrepreneurship, team work, and their work ethic that gives them that sharp keen edge in competitiveness.

- Those with good minds to be scholars should also be inventors, innovators, venture capitalists, and entrepreneurs; they must bring new products and services to the market to enrich the lives of people everywhere.

- You must be disciplined enough to think on your own and to seek to excel without someone breathing down your neck.

- There is no reason why third world leaders cannot succeed… if they can maintain social order, educate their people, maintain peace with their neighbors, and gain the confidence of investors by upholding the rule of law.

- The world owes you nothing. Get up on your feet and challenge yourself to solve the problems of your nation. Complains have not and will not solve our problems. Instead of tasking our minds to innovatively and creatively solve these problems will.

CHAPTER 6

BE THE GOOD NEWS

Will I be wrong to say, while we are busy complaining in Africa, Singapore, on the other hand, was busy taking responsibility for their problems and innovatively solving these problems? No wonder the country is recognized for her prominence today. Most Africans want the government to do this and that as if we are not humans. One of the most significant factors that make you human is your ability to provide answers. We are not even been taught or encouraged to provide answers. We are not even been challenged to be solution providers. We are not even been challenged to take on the issues head on. We are not even been told that that's what we are here for.

> *Let us not seek the Republican answer or the Democratic answer, but the right answer. Let us not seek to fix the blame for the past. Let us accept our own responsibility for the future.*
> JOHN F. KENNEDY

I couldn't agree less with the words of J. F. Kennedy here. We can't do anything about our past, but the future is tied to what we do today. As we face the future, I will like us to emulate individuals who have taken responsibility to address one or more problems for Africans or in Africa.

Here are just a few of them for you:

HARRIET TUBMAN, nicknamed "Moses" referring to the Biblical character who escaped slavery — The Slave who saved other slaves

Harriet Tubman (1822 – 10 March 1913) was an escaped slave who became a leading figure in the abolitionist movement. She also served as a spy for the US army during the civil war and was an active participant in the struggle for women's suffrage.

She was frequently whipped by her overseers — leading to scars which would last all her life. On one occasion, Tubman was hit in the head by a stone thrown by a slave owner. The slave owner was aiming at another slave, but the stone hit Tubman in the back of her head — cracking her skull and leading to lifelong headaches, epileptic seizures and dreams/visions.

In 1849, Tubman's slave owner died and she decided to escape. The escape was successful. Tubman took on odd jobs to earn some money, but she wanted to return to Maryland to rescue others, despite realizing the dangers, this was a cause she was willing to lose her life for.

In her words — "I had crossed the line of which I had so long been dreaming. I was free; but there was no one to welcome me to the land of freedom, I was a stranger in a strange land, and my home after all was down in the old cabin quarter, with the old folks, and my brothers and sisters. But *to this solemn resolution, I came; I was free, and they should be free also; I would make a home for them in the North, and the Lord helping me, I would bring them all there."*

This task of retrieving slaves was made more difficult by the Fugitive Slave Law of 1850, which heavily punished anyone helping slaves to escape — even in states which outlawed slavery.

Tubman helped rescue over 70 slaves, in about 13 expeditions (and offering advice to much more). She often travelled in the darker winter months, making it easier to travel incognito by night. Because of the dangers on the road, she always took a revolver with her. She was also willing to use it to threaten any escaped slave who wished to go back because she knew returning would endanger all the escapees. She was proud never to lose an escaping slave on her expeditions. However, because of her exploits, she earned the nickname "Moses" referring to the Biblical character who escaped slavery and came back to save the others.

> *I was the conductor of the Underground Railroad for eight years, and I can say what most conductors can't say — I never ran my train off the track and I never lost a passenger."*
> HARRIET TUBMAN

Frederick Douglas, who was a noted activist against slavery, praised Tubman for her role in helping slaves. In particular, he praised her courage and willingness to work without recognition. He said of Tubman:

Problems your shortcut to prominence

"Excepting John Brown — of sacred memory — I know of no one who has willingly encountered more perils and hardships to serve our enslaved people than you have"

A big element of Tubman's life was her strong religious faith. She related receiving strong visions and clear messages coming from God, and on the dangerous missions, she trusted in the guidance and protection of God to succeed in her mission.

Harriet Tubman has become an icon symbol of courage and resistance to injustice, inspiring many generations of civil rights activists. In April 2016, it was announced she would figure on the US $20 bill.

Just before you go to the next inspiring story of Rosa Parks, who refused to give up her sit on a public bus to solve the problem of racial discrimination and injustice, I will like you to consider this.

Can God trust you enough to be a solution to that problem? In what areas of life does the Lord not have to bother because you are there? Are you willing to solve a problem not minding the cost or your personal problems? Harriet Tubman was a slave that saved other slaves and risking her life in the process. What about the banking and finance sector; the educational sector, the entertainment industry, can God trust you to be an answer there?

ROSA PARKS,
"Mother of the Modern-Day Civil Rights Movement"

> *There shall be no solution to this race problem until you, yourselves, strike the blow for liberty.*
> MARCUS GARVEY

Rosa Louise McCauley Parks (1913–2005) was an African American civil right activist and seamstress whom the U.S. Congress dubbed the "Mother of the Modern-Day Civil Rights Movement".

Parks is famous for her refusal on December 1, 1955, to obey bus driver James Blake's demand that she relinquish her seat to a white man. Her subsequent arrest and trial for this act of civil disobedience triggered the Montgomery Bus Boycott, one of the largest and most successful mass movements against racial segregation in history, and launched Martin Luther King Jr., one of the organizers of the boycott, to the forefront of the civil rights movement. Her role in American history earned her an iconic status in American culture, and her actions have left an enduring legacy for civil rights movements around the world.

As a child, Rosa became aware of the segregation which was deeply embedded in Alabama. She experienced deep rooted racism and became aware of the different opportunities faced by white and black children. This was a problem to her and she decided to do something about it. Due to the Jim Crow laws, most black voters were effectively disenfranchised.

"I WAS TIRED OF GIVING IN"

In 1900, Montgomery had passed a city ordinance for the purpose of segregating passengers by race. Over time and by custom, however, Montgomery bus drivers had adopted the practice of requiring black riders to move whenever there were no white only seats left.

So, following standard practice, the bus driver demanded that four black people give up their seats in the middle section so that the white passengers could sit. The other three people moved, but I didn't.

Years later, in recalling the events of the day, Parks said, "When that white driver stepped back toward us, when he waved his hand and ordered us up and out of our seats, I felt a determination cover my body like a quilt on a winter night."

She also detailed her motivation in her autobiography, My Story:

"People always say that I didn't give up my seat because I was tired, but that isn't true. I was not tired physically, or no more tired than I usually was at the end of a working day. I was not old, although some people have an image of me as being old then. I was forty-two. No, the only tired I was, was tired of giving in."

When Parks refused to give up her seat, a police officer arrested her. On Sunday, December 4, 1955, plans for the Montgomery Bus Boycott were announced at black churches in the area. At a church rally that night, attendees unanimously agreed to continue the boycott until they were treated with the level of courtesy they expected until black drivers were hired, and until seating in the middle of the bus was handled on a first-come basis.

IT'S TIME TO SOLVE THAT PROBLEM

Parks recalled:

"I did not want to be mistreated; I did not want to be deprived of a seat that I had paid for. It was just time… there was an opportunity for me to take a stand to express the way I felt about being treated in that manner. I had not planned to get arrested. I had plenty to do without having to end up in jail. But when I had to face that decision, I didn't hesitate to do so because I felt that we had endured that too long. The more we gave in, the more we complied with that kind of treatment, the more oppressive it became."

My dear friend, It's time to wake and solve that problem once and for all. If people like this can stand up to face a problem and be a solution to the cries of many, are you any different? Don't give in any longer. It's time.

The day of Parks' trial about 35,000 leaflets was distributed, which read, "We are…asking every Negro to stay off the buses Monday in protest of the arrest and trial… You can afford to stay out of school for one day. If you work, take a cab, or walk. But please, children and grown-ups, don't ride the bus at all on Monday. Please stay off the buses Monday."

It rained that day, but the black community persevered in their boycott. About 40,000 black commuters walked, some as far as 20 miles. In the end, the boycott lasted for 382 days. Dozens of public buses stood idle for months, severely damaging the bus transit company's finances until the law requiring segregation on public buses was lifted.

Some segregationists retaliated with terrorism. Black churches were burned or dynamited. Martin Luther King's home was also bombed. However, the black community's bus boycott marked one of the largest and most successful mass movements against racial segregation. It sparked many other protests, and it catapulted King to the forefront of the Civil Rights Movement.

Through her role in sparking the boycott, Rosa Parks played an important part in internationalizing the awareness of the plight of African Americans and the civil rights struggle.

After the boycott, Rosa Parks became an icon and leading spokesperson of the civil rights movement in the US.

Some of the awards Rosa Parks received.

- She was selected to be one of the people to meet Nelson Mandela on his release from prison in 1994.
- In 1996, she was awarded the Presidential Medal of Freedom from President Bill Clinton
- In 1997, she was awarded the Congressional Gold Medal — the highest award of Congress.

ALIKO DANGOTE,
Richest African and black man on the planet

> *I built a conglomerate and emerged the richest black man in the world in 2008 but it didn't happen overnight. It took me 30 years to get to where I am today. Youths of today aspire to be like me but they want to achieve it overnight. It's not going to work. To build a successful business, you must start small and dream big. In the journey of entrepreneurship, the tenacity of purpose is supreme.*
>
> ALIKO DANGOTE

Aliko Dangote represents what African businessmen should be. He is an example for aspiring entrepreneurs across the continent. He was awarded Nigeria's second highest honor, Grand Commander of the Order of the Niger (GCON) by the President of Nigeria, Goodluck Jonathan making him one of the 10 individuals to be given the honor till date.

He started out as a trader of commodities, became Africa's leading businessman, with companies in 16 countries, employing over 10,000 people. In the process, he became the richest African and black man on the planet. It is this feat that makes him eminently qualified and deservingly recognized as the Vanguard Newspaper African Personality of the Year.

That was not the case in Kano, Nigeria when Aliko Dangote was born. He was just like any other kid. He, like other children, learnt to crawl, walk, run and cried like others. But unlike others, he had always, as all real entrepreneurs do, seen opportunities where others see high risk and failure. In an atmosphere of difficulty, when others would have given up, he took the risk.

He started as a commodity trader, he made a success of it, he entered into sugar refining, and he made a success of it. He set up cement manufacturing; he has made a huge success of it. Now he is venturing into petroleum product refining. Don't be deceived, the success is tied to the fact that he was solving a problem no one paid attention to in the country.

His hard work has set him apart to the envy of his detractors who only see him as a beneficiary of government waiver and concession. But there are others who have had the same benefit but could not make anything tangible from it.

That has brought success to him, his family, state, country, and continent. He has invested in the various sectors of the Nigerian economy and across the African continent thus creating millions of direct and indirect jobs in the continent of Africa. He has become a business colossus that bestrides the global business environment, making him the richest African today.

Dangote owns the Obajana Cement plant which is the largest cement manufacturing facility in Africa. He is also exploring the telecommunications sector and has started building 14,000 kilometers of fiber optic cables to supply the whole of Nigeria and as a result, he was honored in January 2009 as the leading provider of employment in the Nigerian construction industry.

He is also establishing a $100 million truck assembly plant in Lagos, Nigeria in a move that is expected to create about 3,000 jobs. The plant, which is located in Ikeja, has the capacity to produce 10,000 trucks annually. Dangote Group also plans to expand the project in future to meet the national truck demand and export to other African countries to generate foreign exchange for Nigeria.

Apart from his business acumen, he is also a philanthropist who has collaborated with American billionaire, Bill Gates Foundation to invest in the provision of health especially the eradication of polio in Africa and other parts of the world where the disease is still prevalent.

The Foundation contributed $500,000 (N79.15 million) through the United Nations Children's Fund (UNICEF) to support the Federal Government's response to a recent measles outbreak that affected many states in Nigeria. $6.4 million towards building a world class International Cancer Centre in Abuja, in 2009 and another $2.6 million (N430 million) to victims of the flood disaster and for women empowerment in Kogi State.

What are the problems you have chosen to resolve? What are the problems you have decided to bring solutions to? What are the problems you have decided to eradicate in your nation? What problems will cease to exists because of you?

This will also take us to the story of Dr. Innocent Chukwuma who like his colleague, Dangote, has been thriving in solving the problem of unemployment in the country of

Nigeria through their entrepreneurial skills. They have also been instrumental in projecting a positive image for the country abroad.

Here comes the story of a man who wants to eradicate the use of second-hand cars in the country and make his countrymen drive brand new cars suited for the continent's climate at an affordable price.

DR. INNOCENT CHUKWUMA, the Henry Ford of Nigeria

Dr. Innocent Chukwuma, popularly known as Innoson, is the group Chairman and CEO of Innoson Vehicles Manufacturing (IVM) Co. Ltd, the first indigenous vehicle manufacturing plant in Nigeria.

Presently, the company has made in-road into some African countries such as Ghana, Sierra Leone, Chad, Niger, Togo. As the first indigenous motor manufacturing company in Nigeria, he says he wanted to prove that Nigerians can do it. This he says has been proved. According to him, the inspiration to go into vehicle manufacturing was drawn from a desire to see Nigerians drive new cars.

According to him in an interview with Vanguard, he says "Nigeria has become a dumping ground for second hand cars. I know it was the high price of new vehicles that made Nigerians resort to patronizing old vehicles, but since we decided to manufacture the vehicles here, the price is affordable, and our people can drive new vehicles again"

Due to his group of manufacturing companies, he has ensured employment of more than 7,400 Nigerians who work in the company's factory and are all on his payroll.

Seventy per cent (70%) of all materials used to produce these cars are now manufactured in Nigeria.

He has singled out himself to solve the problem of unemployment for about 7,400 youths. He has also given Nigerians and West Africa a chance to drive brand new cars, thereby creating a positive image for the continent, contrary to the dumping ground for used vehicles.

You who are reading this now, I want you to know that as an individual, it is not a mistake that you are a Nigerian, African or a citizen of any country. It is not a mistake that God brought you into this world from that part of the world.

It is because God has put the answer to at least one of the myriads of problems facing your country in you. And my goal with this book is to stir you up to action. My dream is to get you up and running dishing out that solution that is inside you. These ones should be our models as we seek to rebuild our nation and continent.

BISHOP DESMOND TUTU, Archbishop (RT) — South Africa

Desmond Mpilo Tutu was born on 7 October 1931 in South Africa. As a vocal and committed opponent of apartheid in South Africa, he was awarded the Nobel Peace Prize in 1984.

The retired, Anglican Bishop, Desmond Tutu, continues to influence global discourse on various matters pertaining to political and social injustices in Africa. He remains the must-go-to revered figure for advice from even the world's most powerful politicians, like Barack Obama and so does Charlize Theron.

CAMPAIGN AGAINST APARTHEID

In 1976, there were increasing levels of protests by black South Africa against apartheid, especially in Soweto. In his position as a leading member of the clergy, Desmond Tutu used his influence to speak strongly and unequivocally against apartheid, often comparing it to Fascist regimes.

> *If you are neutral in situations of injustice, you have chosen the side of the oppressor. If an elephant has its foot on the tail of a mouse and you say that you are neutral, the mouse will not appreciate your neutrality.*
> DESMOND TUTU

His outspoken criticism caused him to be briefly jailed in 1980 and his passport was twice revoked. However, due in part to his position in the church, the government were reluctant to make a 'martyr' out of him.

Tutu is one of the patrons of The Forgiveness Project, a UK-based charity which seeks to facilitate conflict resolution and break the cycle of vengeance and retaliation.

> *Do your little bit of good where you are; it's those little bits of good put together that overwhelm the world.*
> DESMOND TUTU

Tutu was the first black ordained South African Anglican Archbishop of Cape Town. Other awards given to Desmond Tutu include The Gandhi Peace Prize in 2007, the Albert Schweitzer Prize for Humanitarianism, and the Magubela prize for liberty in 1986

> *I don't preach a social gospel; I preach the Gospel, period. The gospel of our Lord Jesus Christ is concerned for the whole person. When people were hungry, Jesus didn't say, "Now is that political or social?" He said, "I feed you." Because the good news to a hungry person is bread.*
> DESMOND TUTU

The anti-apartheid hero will always be proof that religious leaders can use their influence to make a real difference in the world. This was the problem he dedicated his life to resolving. He went to prison for it, but he still strongly defended this cause. This was his good news to his people. Trust me on this, if you are a solution to a problem affecting a group of people — You become their good news. Is your life good news?

IS YOUR LIFE GOOD NEWS?

Harriet Tubman was good news to the slaves. Rosa Parks was good news to the African Americans dying silently from racial discrimination. Aliko Dangote and Innocent Chukwuma are good news to the thousands of unemployed youths and those children suffering from various health issues. Is your life good news to your nation?

The educational sector is still waiting for their good news. The entertainment industry awaits innovative solutions. Science and technology, Banking and finance await the answers that are locked up in your bosom. You are a problem solver. And this problem is your shortcut to prominence.

Though Singapore moved from a third world nation to a first world nation in a matter of 50 years, her problems did not disappear. Individuals like you and I took up the challenge to address different problems in different fields.

I will be elaborating more on the practical steps you can take to begin making a difference big time in the following chapters. Meanwhile, in the next chapter, I will show you a few out of the billions of potentials that problems hold for you. My dear friend, become a problem solver that is your shortcut to prominence.

It is my conviction that if you apply this model and pick lessons from these individuals, while others are complaining, you will be making tremendous progress.

NUGGETS

- Can God trust you enough to be a solution to that problem? In what areas of life does the Lord not have to bother because you are there?

- Dangote started as a commodity trader, he made a success of it, he entered into sugar refining, and he made a success of it. He set up cement manufacturing; he has made a huge success of it. Now he is venturing into petroleum product refining. Don't be deceived, the success is tied to the fact that he was solving a problem no one paid attention to in the country.

- God has put the answer to at least one of the myriads of problems facing your country in you.

- If you are neutral in situations of injustice, you have chosen the side of the oppressor. If an elephant has its foot on the tail of a mouse and you say that you are neutral, the mouse will not appreciate your neutrality.

- Do your little bit of good where you are; it's those little bits of good put together that overwhelm the world.

- If you are a solution to a problem affecting a group of people — You become their good news.

CHAPTER 7

FOCUS ON THE SOLUTION

In opening this chapter, I will like to elucidate a little more on what I mean by being 'the Good News.' From the previous chapter, you already saw a few examples of individuals who lay down their lives, wealth, hard work, and excellence to bring solutions to problems facing their land.

This will take us back in time to the biblical story of Caleb and Joshua, two of the twelve spies sent by Moses to spy the Promised Land and bring reports about what sort of land it was. They were to tell everyone what the place looked like.

> "And the Lord spake unto Moses, saying, Send thou men, that they may search the land of Canaan, which I give unto the children of Israel: of every tribe of their fathers shall ye send a man, everyone a ruler among them."
> NUMBERS 13:1-2 (KJV)

When they returned, ten of the twelve spies came with a discouraging report of how impossible it is to take over the land. They perfectly analyzed the problem and how impossible it is to ever surmount the challenge of inheriting the Promised Land.

These ten are like the majority of Africans today, they know the problems, and they can analyze the challenges and the pitfalls of the government, but more importantly, they don't see these problems been solved. They don't have an iota of hope that these problems can ever be solved. They kind of have a magnifying lens that only increases the size of the problem and makes it look insurmountable.

> *[32] And they brought up an evil report of the land which they had searched unto the children of Israel, saying, The land, through which we have gone to search it, is a land that eateth up the inhabitants thereof; and all the people that we saw in it are men of a great stature. [33] And there we saw the giants, the sons of Anak, which come of the giants: and we were in our own sight as grasshoppers, and so we were in their sight.*
> NUMBERS 13:32-33 (KJV)

These ten men already gave up on the problem. They magnified the problem to the status of a giant and all they could see of themselves is as small as a grasshopper. So, to them, this is a mission impossible!

And I believe this is the wrong attitude we have towards problems today. This is the wrong mentality we've been fed with. That's the reason why the only thing you see is how bad and hopeless the situation is.

Focus On The Solution

You can talk and talk about how bad the power supply is, in the country or the rate of corruption. You analyze the deplorable situation of the educational sector and the lack of honesty and integrity in our banking and finance sector or the values that have been lost in our entertainment industry.

But here is what I want you to understand that if you will challenge yourself, add value to yourself, educate and build up yourself, you are well able to handle any challenge that may come your way. You have the capacity to deal decisively with every problem that has befallen your nation. And it is time you began to do something in this regard. Begin to see problems from a different world view.

HAVE A DIFFERENT WORLDVIEW

While every other person saw the problems, there were these other individuals who saw things differently — Caleb and Joshua. Though they saw the same things the other ten men saw, their interpretation was quite different. They saw the problem quite alright but that was not the only thing they envisioned.

> *And Caleb stilled the people before Moses, and said, Let us go up at once, and possess it; for we are well able to overcome it."*
> **Numbers 13:30 (KJV)**

This was the same land the other spies saw. This is the kind of attitude that births solutions. This is the good news to the Israelites who wanted to inherit the Promised Land.

This is the worldview that will save the epileptic power supply in Africa. This is the mindset that will rescue our nations from the claws of corruption. This is the point of view that will make poverty a surmountable mountain. This is the only way to maximize our potentials. This is the mindset of problem solvers.

Don't get me wrong here; I totally understand the deplorable state of things on the African continent right now. I am an African man, a Nigerian for that matter, even though I don't live in Africa. And I will prove this to you.

So, let's take the case of power supply as an example, because that has been the excuse for most people for years. That's why you hear people say things like, "the economy of the continent of Africa is growing rapidly, but one significant problem persists — a shortage in electrical capacity."

HOW BAD IS AFRICA'S ELECTRICITY PROBLEM?

Out of the 48 countries of Sub-saharan Africa (with a combined population of more than 750 million), it only generates roughly the same amount of power as Spain (a single country of fewer than 50 million people).

Our continent has arguably the worst electric power infrastructure in the world with the lowest scores in power generation, consumption, and security of supply! Electricity supply in Africa is in a very sorry state. Millions of Africans now have mobile phones with no electricity to charge batteries.

In many countries on the continent, less than 20 percent of the populations have access to electricity; the situation is much worse in rural areas where fewer than 5 percent are connected to the grid.

According to this New York Times article which featured a story about one Mr. John, a Nigerian rural farmer (like many others in his village), who had to take a 3-hour taxi ride to charge his cellphone batteries in the nearest town with electricity. The number of people doing the same thing in surrounding villages was so high that many of them had to leave their phones behind at the charging center (for up to three days) before returning to pick them.

To fight the darkness, up to 80 percent of Africans depend on personal generators, candles, and kerosene (paraffin) lamps to provide basic lighting. Let's not even talk about all the other things we desperately need electricity for — iron clothes, pump water, charge mobile phones etc.

According to this World Bank report, the average power consumed per person in Africa every year is only enough to power one 100-watt light bulb for only three hours a day! On average, fewer than three out of 10 Africans have access to electricity. Africa also has the world's lowest annual per capita electricity consumption: 450 kWh.

Those who live through electricity shortages everyday fully understand the scale of this problem. I'm only quoting research reports for the benefit of Africa's elite and people who don't live on the continent like me, who may find it difficult to grasp the severity of Africa's electricity challenges.

We understand that some countries in the region (like South Africa) have it better than the others. In many other countries, it's just terrible!

> *Every problem has in it the seeds of its own solution. If you don't have any problems, you don't get any seeds.*
> NORMAN VINCENT PEALE

Nevertheless, there are a couple of individuals who see these problems as surmountable. They have a different worldview. They've seen the enormous opportunities that lie under this so-called 'big deal.' They know it's their shortcut to prominence.

AKON LIGHTING AFRICA

Though, popularly known as Akon among his fans, his real name is Aliaume Damala Badara Akon Thiam, born in 1973. The famous Senegalese-American singer, songwriter, producer and businessman is known for his R&B-style vocals. According to Forbes, he is one of the most powerful celebrities in Africa.

He lived in Senegal, West Africa, as a child and attended high school in the United States, where he eventually settles. He has since become a voice to be reckoned with in the entertainment industry worldwide.

Akon's Solar Power Initiative aims to bring electricity to 600 Million people in Africa. Despite being best known for making pop music, Akon's decided to give filling dance floors a break in favor of bringing solar energy to people living in rural Africa. This isn't just another charitable celebrity contribution. This might be the most ambitious charitable endeavor ever.

R&B singer Akon has launched an initiative aiming to bring electricity to 600 million people in Africa. The *Akon Lighting Africa* initiative has started the Solar Academy, which will help African engineers harness the sun's energy to produce electricity for the target of 600 million people.

Considering that Africa gets an average of 320 sunny days in a given calendar year, this plan more than makes sense. But to say it's extensive and ambitious would be a giant understatement.

The Academy will teach African residents how to install and maintain solar-powered electricity systems and micro grids to continually produce electricity.

> *We have the sun and innovative technologies to bring electricity to homes and communities. We now need to consolidate African expertise.*
> SAMBA BAITHILY, A CO-FOUNDER OF THE PROJECT, TOLD REUTERS

The hope is that the continent's population — 70 percent of which is under the age of 35 — will help boosts the economy, provide opportunities to future generations and just flat-out increase the overall quality of life.

According to multiple reports, *Akon Lighting Africa* has received a credit line of up to $1 billion from construction juggernaut China Jiangsu International and will begin work with the most low-resource, remote areas.

Problems your shortcut to prominence

Already revered in his native Senegal, Akon's level of love and respect worldwide will sky-rocket if his ambition generates massive results.

- USD 1 billion credit line for launch, from international banks
- 15 countries of operation 480 communities covered
- 100,000 solar street lamps
- 1,200 solar micro-grids
- 102,000 solar domestic kits
- 75,000$ per village on average
- 5,500 indirect jobs created

With an estimated 600 million Africans lacking electricity, the initiative is poised to tackle a daunting problem. But they're far from alone in seeking to change lives through this energy source — solar is increasingly seen as both a viable alternative and a business opportunity on the continent.

Yet it's not just Africa that sees the promise of solar power. According to the same report: *"By 2050, analysts from the International Energy Association (IEA) believe the sun could be the world's largest source of power."*

The academy will teach African engineers and entrepreneurs how to produce solar power. European experts will be on hand to help with training and equipment.

In the same light, Google, one of the world's most successful multi-billion dollar corporations recently invested

$12 million in the Jasper Power Plant, a South African solar project. This solar plant is planned to supply nearly 100 Mega Watts of clean energy to the country.

There are also other huge multi-billion dollar investments like the DESERTEC project that plans to set up solar farms in vast areas of the Sahara desert and supply Europe with the generated electricity.

"It is true that everyone has problems, and it is also true that every problem has a solution. If this is the reality of life, then why not focus on solutions rather than problems."

This is the same problem that nations have not been able to surmount. This is the same problem that nations across the continent have been clueless on how to resolve. Here come individuals who have decided to take this problem head on. They chose not to complain but to solve the problem.

THINK OUTSIDE THE BOX

Visionary people face the same problems everyone else faces; but rather than get paralyzed by their problems, visionaries immediately commit themselves to finding a solution.
BILL HYBELS

So, what did they see differently? With an average of 325 days of bright sunlight every year, solar power remains one of Africa's most abundant but scarcely used resources.

Solar power/electricity is produced when the fancy, silver-colored and shiny sheets (commonly known as 'solar panels' are used to capture and convert the sun's radiation to electricity. These panels (which contain photovoltaic cells) come in different models, shapes, and sizes.

SOLAR ENERGY IS THE FASTEST AND CHEAPEST WAY TO LIGHT UP AFRICA

Thousands of villages in Africa are so remote and too spread apart that it would take decades and billions of investment dollars to take electricity to all corners of our continent.

Small towns and villages that were not considered a priority by governments now have a huge demand for electricity. Mobile phones, which have been widely successful in Africa, have changed the profile of power consumption in Africa. Also, different skilled laborers now need this for their work.

The mobile phone revolution is forcing millions of poor Africans to demand electricity. More people now depend on their mobile phones to contact relatives, obtain general news and information about farm product prices, and make/receive small money transfers.

Africa does not have the kind of investment and political commitment it will require to connect every corner of the continent to the power grid. It's already too late, no matter how fast this is done.

What Africa needs now is an alternative that is *cheap, easy to deploy, decentralized* and *effective* enough to provide electricity to millions of people in the shortest possible time. And this is what these individuals who are thinking outside the box are maximizing.

Of all the other alternative and renewable sources of energy available for Africa's future — wind, sun, and water — the sun (solar power) is the most abundant and free!

Because most of Africa sits on the earth's equator, the sun's radiation reaches many parts of the continent including the remotest parts — villages, mountain tops, anywhere and everywhere! This raw energy already touches the parts of the continent that power grids and infrastructure have still not reached — after many decades!

THE DEMAND FOR CLEANER AND GREENER ALTERNATIVE POWER SOURCES IS GAINING MOMENTUM

A significant portion of electricity generated on our continent is from non-renewable sources like petrol, natural gas, coal and other fossil fuels. These fuels remain expensive and have dangerous effects on our health, the environment, and climate.

In fact, at the current rate of consumption and population growth, Africa's estimated petroleum reserves (roughly 60 billion barrels) is not likely to last for very long.

Africa's solar power potential is so huge and has the capacity to generate and supply electricity to Europe and other parts of the world in the near future.

START FROM WHERE YOU ARE

Now, imagine that while they are thinking outside the box to solve the power issues in the continent, you are doing the same in the industry of commerce and someone else is doing so in the entertainment industry; another person is solving different problems in the educational sector and the judiciary system. Can you now begin to picture the greatness of our continent coming forth?

I hope you are beginning to share the same conviction I have that Africa will no longer be referred to as the *'dark continent?'* But that Africa will become the true definition of greatness. This will only come when we take responsibility for our problems and begin to think outside the box to solve them.

You don't have to be a politician or hold an appointment in the government to begin to solve problems. All you need is the right attitude to these problems. All you have to do is to shun the survival mentality. All that is required of you now is to be a problem solver. Be the good news to your society and this will secure your place in history.

You must identify that area or sector of the land that you are passionate about fixing today. You must also begin from this moment to take steps towards bringing about salvation and deliverance in that sphere of contact. You must begin to confront the problems and challenges there. You must bring about change, growth, development and hope in the sectors of the land that you are concerned about.

Focus On The Solution

*Too often we give children answers to
remember rather than problems to solve.*
ROGER LEWIN

Listen closely, you don't necessarily have to change the whole country or continent but you can start from where you are. Start from your peers and colleagues. Believe that every problem has within it the key to its solution. And begin to seek out problems to solve.

NUGGETS

- If you will challenge yourself, add value to yourself, educate and build up yourself, you are well able to handle any challenge that may come your way.

- It is true that everyone has problems, and it is also true that every problem has a solution. If this is the reality of life, then why not focus on solutions rather than problems.

- You don't have to be a politician or hold an appointment in the government to begin to solve problems. All you need is the right attitude to problems.

- With an average of 325 days of bright sunlight every year, solar power remains one of Africa's most abundant but scarcely used resources.

- You don't necessarily have to change the whole country or continent but you can start from where you are.

CHAPTER 8

YOU ARE HERE TO SOLVE A PROBLEM

There are several people and maybe you inclusive who are of the opinion that they can never be of relevance to national or international development because they aren't politicians or in government. They think that only those elected or appointed to leadership positions have the opportunity to make a difference but that is about to change.

Guess what! Even those elected to these political offices come under the influence of several factors that limit what they can do or what they want to do, even though they have good intentions. And these factors can't really hold you back if you are working as an individual or a Non-governmental organization (NGO).

Every one of us has an important assignment to fulfill here on earth. You are here to solve a problem. God saw a problem and created you to come here to solve it. Find an area where you are passionate about. And begin to identify the problems in that area in a bid to provide solutions to them. Therefore, you should stop thinking you can't do anything to improve things in the land because you are not a politician.

Problems your shortcut to prominence

Come to think of it, do you realize that a large part of your day is being influenced by a few individuals already who are not politicians at all?

Your satellite-enabled alarm clock goes off. Blame Albert Einstein for rousting you out of bed.

You put on the electric bulb. Thanks to Thomas Edison for the electric bulb that can now last for several hours.

You nick yourself shaving and drip toothpaste on your shirt. Blame Einstein for the mess. His creation of a formula to measure the size of molecules dissolved in liquids made it possible for scientists — among many other, more important, leaps — to create or improve thousands of consumer products, including better shaving creams and toothpaste.

You click on the television to check the weather and traffic. It's raining, and the traffic cameras show that the cars are already backed up for miles on the interstate. It's going to be a rough commute. Blame Einstein for your bad mood.

You pick up your phone, tablet or laptop to check and reply your mails. Thanks to Steve Jobs for the smaller and lighter design of computers and Bill Gates for having a vision for the Personal Computers.

You check your Facebook page and you have loads of messages to reply to. Blame Mark Zuckerberg for connecting the world.

You go online and type in any question and the answer comes out. Thanks to Google founders — Larry Page and Sergey Brin.

They are not politicians. In fact, they did not hold any position in government. And for those of them still alive, they've not held any position in government. Yet, they've influenced how billions of people who woke up this morning on earth live their lives. That's the power of thinking outside the box. That's the power of tasking your mind. That's the result of resolving a problem.

Let's pick a few examples from here and you will better understand what I am talking about.

ALBERT EINSTEIN:
Success story of physicist and scientist

A German-born scientist, the inventor of the theory of relativity, whose name has become synonymous with the word "genius" and whose $E=mc^2$ equation is studied by millions of students every year. Not only was he recognized as a prominent physicist and the winner of the 1921 Nobel Prize in Physics, but also as a philosopher, theologian, lifelong pacifist and amateur musician. Yet you are sure to learn many more unexpected sides to his persona throughout the story I will share with you.

EARLY LIFE

Albert Einstein was born on March 14, 1879, in the city of Ulm.

Though now the name Einstein is often used as a synonym to "genius," Albert was not a childhood prodigy. He started speaking relatively late when he was three years old. The scientist himself later commented that at that time he often formed full sentences in his thoughts, but did not utter them.

SCHOOL YEARS

As a student, young Einstein did not show remarkable results. Most of his grades were passing, and he was near the top of his class, but mainly because of math and science. His learning success depended mostly on his interest in the subject. Einstein loved doing things his own way rather than following the teachers' guidelines.

> *The true sign of intelligence is not knowledge but imagination.*
> ALBERT EINSTEIN

The core value of college education according to Einstein was the art of learning how to learn.

ANNUS MIRABILIS PAPERS AND THE MIRACLE YEAR

The year of 1905 is called the "miracle year" of Albert Einstein, while he was still 26 years old. Sometimes it is called the "annus mirabilis," which in Latin means the "miracle year." The reason for this was that he wrote four papers printed in a scientific journal *Annalen der Physik* that contributed significantly to the groundwork of modern physics and completely changed the view of space, time, mass, and energy. More importantly, it revolutionized the way we lived our lives today. Those papers were on the photoelectric effect, Brownian motion, special theory of relativity, and mass-energy equivalence.

THE PHOTOELECTRIC EFFECT

His postulation of the photon (a "particle" of light) and the photoelectric effect — which was described in his first great paper of 1905 and won him the Nobel Prize in 1921 — gave us scores of everyday applications.

The declaration of the photoelectric effect made possible the eventual invention of television cameras. And the remotes that control them. Also, that's the reason why digital cameras work. Compact disc and DVD players use lasers.

BROWNIAN MOTION

On May 11, 1905, Albert Einstein completed his second work titled *On the Movement of Small Particles Suspended in a Stationary Liquids by the Molecular-Kinetic Theory of Heat* delineated a stochastic model of Brownian motion. Special Theory of Relativity

The third paper titled *On the Electrodynamics of Moving Bodies* was received on June 30, 1905, and released on September 26, 1905. It combined Maxwell's equations for electricity and magnetism with the laws of mechanics by introducing fundamental changes to mechanics close to the speed of light. Later it would become the background of Einstein's theory of relativity.

Medical revolutions like the PET scan rest on positrons are possible thanks to this theory.

It was the statement of the quantum effect, without which we would not have cellular telephones or smoke detectors or burglar alarms or those doors that automatically open at the supermarket or on the elevator.

MASS-ENERGY EQUIVALENCE

The paper contained an argument for arguably the most famous equation, $E=mc^2$, in the field of physics. It helped to understand how the sun generates the energy.

Carbon dating — we can take a stab at measuring how old fossils are thanks to Einstein ($E=mc^2$ shows that mass and energy are interconnected; by measuring the degradation of nuclei in atoms of organic materials, the theory goes, we can measure how long they've been degrading).

THE NOBEL PRIZE IN PHYSICS

Only a life lived for others is a life worthwhile.
ALBERT EINSTEIN

Albert Einstein was awarded the 1921 Nobel Prize "for his services to Theoretical Physics, and especially for his discovery of the law of the photoelectric effect."

Albert Einstein died at the age of 76 in Princeton Hospital. Thomas Stoltz Harvey, a doctor at the Princeton Hospital, performed the autopsy and preserved Einstein's brain without the permission of his family for the neuroscience of the future to discover the reason for his intelligence.

You Are Here to Solve a Problem

> *Once we accept our limits, we go beyond them.*
> **Albert Einstein**

Albert Einstein's life story is a vivid example of how one man's biography can change the course of history.

John Rigden, a physicist at Washington University in St. Louis suggested that "the first contribution that Einstein made that dramatically affects our lives was that he did it with the power of his mind."

Einstein "wasn't blessed with experimental data — it was mostly abstract ideas," he said. "That is a distinctive aspect of *homo sapiens*: We have a big brain...

"He is a standard because of what he did. And how he did it."

Stay with me, because in the next chapter I'll elaborate more on the power of the human mind. The human mind is one of the greatest tools to solve problems today. In my own opinion, it is the most powerful tool. This is what was at work in the Wright brothers when the whole world believed that humans can't fly but they believed otherwise. And what is the reality today?

> *When you think there is nothing left to improve on, your business dies, for there is no shortage of innovators.*
> *Bangambiki Habyarimana*

The number one tool to solve problems in this age is found in your mind because it is where your realities are formed. This does not necessarily mean you have to invent something completely new from the scratch, it may be as little or insignificant as just a shift in point of view. It may simply be a matter of seeing the problem from another angle.

Don't worry, just relax, we will discuss more on this interesting topic in the following chapters. Right now, come back to chapter 8. I know you can't wait, but just before we close this chapter, let's take a look at another man, an inventor who was never a politician but revolutionized six different industries. He has successfully changed the way we live our lives today and the way we relate to each other.

STEVE JOBS:
CEO and co-founder of Apple Inc.

Steve Jobs was born on February 24, 1955, in San Francisco. He was an American inventor, entrepreneur, and industrial designer. He was the CEO and co-founder of Apple Inc., CEO and majority shareholder of Pixar Animation Studios, CEO founder and chairman of NeXT Inc., and a member of The Walt Disney Company's board of directors.

His bold ambitions revolutionized six industries: personal computing, animated movies, music, phones, tablet computing, and digital publishing. Upon his passing, many hailed him as the greatest inventor and entrepreneur of our time — comparing his achievements to those of Thomas Edison.

You are here to solve a problem

The distinctive personality traits of Steve Jobs are perseverance, passion, ambition, rebellious nature, confidence (sometimes arrogance), and far-sighted vision.

His Contributions:

> *When you first start off trying to solve a problem, the first solutions you come up with are very complex, and most people stop there. But if you keep going, and live with the problem and peel more layers of the onion off, you can oftentimes arrive at some very elegant and simple solutions. Most people just don't put in the time or energy to get there. We believe that customers are smart, and want objects which are well thought through.*
>
> **Steve Jobs**

Let's have a look on some of Steve Jobs' works which formed the tech-savvy environment we know of. We'll kick off from the yesteryears going to the present.

The first in the line of his contributions would be the Apple II. Long before the affordable computer was born, and probably the tech-savvy generation were even born computers weren't that affordable for the regular person. In fact, businesses can only afford them. However, it was all thanks to Steve Jobs and Steve Wozniak that computers became affordable for home use when they founded Apple in 1976.

Apple II was release a year later in 1977. After that, the rest became history. If a modern tech-guru would have to take a peek at the Apple II, he may scoff at the outdate spec namely the 1-MHz processor and 4 KB RAM — a slow computer in today's standards. But would you believe that this changed everything and helped make everything what it is today?

The second in the lineup may be the multitasking computer called Lisa. Think of it as the current Macbook's great, great grandmother.

> *Apple took the edge off the word 'computer'*
> STEVE JOBS

Roll in to the last years of the 20th century and we find ourselves transitioning from the diskettes and floppy disks to the circular, storage devices we are highly familiar with right now — and that is the compact disk (CD). The iMac, when it was released in 1998, paved the way for the modern digital era as it was the first to shift from disk-drives to CD-ROM. Aside from that, the iMac was the first to be the internet-ready computer available. Plus it was the first out of the many models to be a stylish computer with its colored and curved edges.

> *If you can't make it good, at least make it look good.*
> BILL GATES

Soon after, Steve Jobs became another contender in another area, which is mobile phones. Mobile phones have become not only a highly coveted accessory but also a necessity as well. The first iPhone was released in 2007 and featured a whole new outlook when it comes to mobile phones. Look at where it is now.

YOU ARE HERE TO SOLVE A PROBLEM

Finally, the last contribution that Steve Jobs made before his untimely passing changed the interface of computers ever since. With the demand for smaller, lighter and handier laptops he introduced the iPad in 2010 which was a tablet computer.

Steve Jobs had a term to his products: magical. Absurd as it may sound, it does have its own sense of logic. His contributions to the technological world are indeed magical as they helped pave the way to the modern 21st century.

> *Being the richest man in the cemetery doesn't matter to me. Going to bed at night saying we've done something wonderful, that's what matters to me.*
> **STEVE JOBS**

Steve Jobs was the man who re-invented the computer world. He managed to take many ground-breaking ideas and implement them into the reality. Steve Jobs' life story was exciting, while at the same time it could not be called an easy one. He faced many obstacles on his life path, but he tackled them with the pride and innovative thinking.

With these examples, I think it's pretty obvious that you don't necessarily have to be in government to solve problems. Better still, you don't have to occupy any leadership position to significantly affect lives with the problems you solve.

See yourself as a solution because that is what you are. You are here to solve problems. There is a problem only you can solve. There is an issue only you can resolve better than anyone else. There is something you are passionate about and you know you can improve that sphere of life.

Don't think less of yourself. Go out there and cause the change. Go out there and make the impact. Task your brain. Use your mind. It is your God-given tool to solve complex problems. Think outside the box. Shun the status quo.

Definitely, this book will not be complete if I fail to tell you how to use your most powerful tool in solving problems. That is exactly what the next chapter will try to help you do. So, don't stop here!

If you truly want to be prominent, you can't stop here, because it is only the problems that you solve that guarantee your prominence. And the place to start causing that change and proffering solutions is right in your mind. You don't necessarily need positions or offices to achieve this, even though it might be an added advantage.

NUGGETS

- God saw a problem and created you to come here to solve it.

- Find an area where you are passionate about. And begin to identify the problems in that area in a bid to provide solutions to them.

- Only a life lived for others is a life worthwhile.

- The number one tool to solve problems in this age is found in your mind because it is where your realities are formed.

- You don't have to occupy any leadership position to significantly affect lives with the problems you solve.

- See yourself as a solution because that is what you are.

- There is a problem only you can solve. There is an issue only you can resolve better than anyone else.

CHAPTER 9

THE POWER OF YOUR MIND

> *Each one of us has all the wisdom and knowledge we ever need right within us. It is available to us through our intuitive mind, which is our connection with universal intelligence.*
>
> SHAKTI GAWAIN

Flash back a few chapters where we discussed the survival mentality. You will recall that I made mention of the fact that what makes us different is our ability to solve problems. What makes us different from animals is the fact that we could provide solutions. It is the fact that we could resolve issues and problems. That is what makes us be superior to animals.

Animals are only concerned about what they will eat, drink, sleep, wake up and sometimes they mate. In essence, they live by their instincts, reflexes or stimuli to meet their immediate needs. Animals tend to use only their God-given abilities and are generally not capable of gaining any more leverage. These are the animal standards of living; Instinct, reflexes, and stimulus. That is why animals eventually lost their natural advantages over humans and humans took over the planet. What do I mean by advantages here?

In the beginning, animals could run faster than humans, but today humans can travel faster and further than animals because they created tools or machines such as bicycle, cars, trucks, trains and planes. Also, in the beginning, birds could fly and humans could not. Today, humans fly higher, further, and faster than any bird. So what happened between then and now? What did humans do differently?

Humans have gained more of an advantage over animals simply because humans have a mind and have put it to work. The same thing happens when some humans use their mind more than other humans. People who use their mind have become prominent and those that refuse to use their mind have remained mediocre. In other words, just as humans gained advantages over animals by putting their mind to use, similarly, humans who use their mind have become more prominent and significant than those who did not.

For better understanding, a bird utilizes its God-given wings as its unique peculiarity to fly. Humans observed birds in flight and then used their minds to discover how humans could also fly. A cheetah uses its legs to run as fast as it could, humans observed this and then used their minds to develop the car, train, bicycle and every other means of transportation.

The people who are not learning to task their mind to proffer solutions are falling behind. The nations who are not bothered about coming up with solutions to their problems are also falling behind. While those who have mastered the art of questioning their mind and putting it to work is moving ahead.

Because of the technology that came from human minds, we have different choices in transportation than our ancestors. Today, instead of just walking, we have the choice of riding a bicycle, driving a car, or flying a plane. Or we might choose to use the television, telephone, or email to span the distances. All these choices provided by these devices were developed in the mind first as a solution to a problem. My dear friend, there is power in your mind to solve any, I mean any problem.

WHY SOME PEOPLE CAN AND OTHERS CAN'T

The Philistine army had gathered for war against Israel. The two armies faced each other, camped for battle on opposite sides of a steep valley. A Philistine giant measuring over nine feet tall and wearing full armor came out each day for forty days, mocking and challenging the Israelites to fight. His name was Goliath. Saul, the King of Israel, and the whole army were terrified of Goliath.

Saul was not just a king, he was a skilled warrior. But Goliath was able to put fear in the whole army of a nation by playing on their minds. He was far taller than any of the Israeli army and covered all over with armor. So, the king and all his army could not see any possibility to defeat this warrior. This was a problem that was too big for them to fathom a way out.

The only problem with their minds was the fact that all they ever knew about war was to fight physically and since none of the armies could match Goliath in their physical appearance they gave up and they were terrified. It was unfortunate that they couldn't think outside the box. They were trained physically, but their minds were not trained. They were only trained to solve problems physically.

I tell you this, new problems will emerge every now and then. And the old solution might be obsolete. Therefore, you need to prepare your mind to always think outside the box. Your mind must be prepared to always think solutions and answers.

> *Thinking is the hardest work there is, which is probably the reason why so few engage in it.*
> HENRY FORD

Only very few engage in this exercise of thinking. As a result, a lot of people can't come up with any solution. Instead, the wrong attitude and the mindset that problems are bad begin to thrive. Therefore, when a new problem surfaces, they conclude that it can't be solved.

I bet you, you will see reasons why a problem cannot be solved. You will see reasons why many have been running away from the problems you are trying to solve. And trust me, these reasons will be logical enough to make you give up on coming up with a solution. This is the simple reason why so many can't and will not attempt solving problems. They've not trained their minds.

Many people are unsuccessful in life because they run when they meet Goliath. Without Goliath, David would never have become a giant of a man.

QUESTION YOUR MIND

One day David, the youngest son of Jesse, was sent to the battle lines by his father to bring back news of his brothers. David was probably just a young teenager at the time. While there, David heard Goliath shouting his daily defiance, and he saw the great fear stirred within the men of Israel. David responded, *"Who is this uncircumcised Philistine that he should defy the armies of God?"*

This is a trained mind talking here."

> *Some men see things as they are and say, "Why?" I dream things that never were and say, "Why not?"*
> ROBERT KENNEDY

Having a mind that can expand its reality or context quickly is an important form of leverage. In fact, it may be your most important form of leverage, especially in this rapidly changing world. This is the mind that questions the status quo. It is a matter of going beyond the confines of what you think is possible in your current realities and into the realm of new possibilities.

David saw the fear in the men of Israel, but he chose to question the status quo. He saw the problem quite alright, but he believed they can come up with a solution. Therefore, he asked a question *"Who is this uncircumcised Philistine that he should defy the armies of God?"*

Likewise, you've got to question your mind. The first thing to do when you see a problem is to question your mind. The *'Problem'* is not really the problem. Even if the problem is a giant; even if the problem is overwhelming; even if it has not been done before; what matters most is what you've trained your mind to do when a new problem surfaces that you are unfamiliar with.

So David volunteered to fight Goliath. It took some persuasion, but King Saul finally agreed to let David fight against the giant.

Dressed in his simple tunic, carrying his shepherd's staff, sling and a pouch full of stones, David approached Goliath. The giant cursed at him, hurling threats and insults.

David said to the Philistine, "You come against me with sword and spear and javelin, but I come against you in the name of the Lord Almighty, the God of the armies of Israel, whom you have defied … today I will give the carcasses of the Philistine army to the birds of the air … and the whole world will know that there is a God in Israel … it is not by sword or spear that the Lord saves; for the battle is the Lord's, and he will give all of you into our hands."

What a man? Sorry, what a boy! Because he was just seventeen years old when he fought Goliath. Though he was a young man physically, his mind was that of a giant.

> *When the Philistine looked around and saw David, he derided and disparaged him because he was [just] a young man, with a ruddy complexion, and a handsome appearance.*
> 1 SAMUEL 17:42 (AMP)

As Goliath moved in for the kill, David reached into his bag and slung one of his stones at Goliath's head. Finding a hole in the armor, the stone sank into the giant's forehead, and he fell face down on the ground. David then took Goliath's sword, killed him and then cut off his head. When the Philistines saw that their hero was dead, they turned and ran. So the Israelites pursued, chasing and killing them and plundering their camp.

POINTS OF INTEREST FROM THE STORY OF DAVID AND GOLIATH

- Why did they wait 40 days to begin the battle? Probably for several reasons. Everyone was afraid of Goliath. He seemed invincible. Not even King Saul, the tallest man in Israel, had stepped out to fight. Also, the sides of the valley were very steep. Whoever made the first move would have a strong disadvantage and probably suffer great loss.

Fear is a thing of the mind. Instead of responding to problems with fear, train your mind to think of solutions when a problem arises. David was just a shepherd, he was not trained at war, but he came up with a solution for a whole nation.

There might be problems in your nation right now that everybody has given up on. Do the opposite, instead of giving in, question the status quo. Question your mind. Come up with a solution.

- David chose not to wear the King's armor because it felt cumbersome and unfamiliar. David was comfortable with his simple sling, a weapon he was skilled at using. God will use the unique skills he's already placed in your hands, so don't worry about "wearing the King's armor." Just be yourself and question your mind. Use the familiar gifts and talents God has given you. Nevertheless, be prepared by refining and polishing those skills before you face the problem. When the problem comes, it might be too late to prepare.

> *By failing to prepare, you are preparing to fail.*
> BENJAMIN FRANKLIN

- David's faith in God caused him to look at the giant from a different perspective. Goliath was merely a mortal man defying an all-powerful God. David looked at the battle from God's point of view. If we look at giant problems and impossible situations from God's perspective, we realize that God will fight for us and with us. When we put things in proper perspective, we see more clearly, and we can fight more effectively.

- When the giant criticized, insulted, and threatened, David didn't stop or even waver. Everyone else cowered in fear, but David ran to the battle. He knew that action needed to be taken. David did the right thing in spite of discouraging insults and fearful threats. Only God's opinion mattered to David.

The Power of Your Mind

Are you facing a giant problem or impossible situation? Stop for a minute and refocus. Can you see the situation more clearly from God's vantage point? Do you need to take courageous action in the face of insults and fearful circumstances? Do you trust that God will fight for you and with you?

DIFFERENCE BETWEEN WINNERS AND LOSERS

What I've learned is that for most people, success is no accident. Winners are winners for a reason just as losers are losers for a reason.

1. **Winners do things losers won't do:** Oftentimes, it's the people who go to almost unthinkable lengths who manage to make it to the top.

Thomas Edison reportedly tried more than 1000 different substances as filaments before he found the right one for the light bulb. Henry Morton Stanley, who was one of the greatest explorers in human history, nearly died time and time again going on expeditions across Africa that took years under some of the most dangerous and miserable conditions imaginable.

Ross Perot and his wife both worked and then they lived off his salary while they saved every cent of her salary to fund his new business. These are people who went to extraordinary lengths to reach the top and they did it instead of complaining that life is hard and giving up.

Also, while winners concentrate and focus all their attention on the possible solution to a problem, losers, on the other hand, focuses on the problem and magnify it. While everyone was concentrating on the strength, height, and armor of Goliath, David chose to see the solution in this situation.

2. **Winners are optimistic while losers are pessimistic**: Both optimists and pessimists tend to think their view of the world is more "realistic." That's because whether you're optimistic or pessimistic, you're probably right. That makes sense if you think about it. If you expect to fail and have a setback, then it's all too easy to say, "I knew it wouldn't work," and give up.

On the other hand, if you expect to succeed and things go badly, then you're much more likely to just shrug it off and keep going forward. As Richard Bach has said,

3. **Winners know what they're trying to do while losers go with the flow**: This one is a little trickier than the other items on the list because after all, not every successful person has mapped out his future. Moreover, there are plenty of successful people who ended up taking their first steps toward success and prosperity without realizing the path that they were on.

That being said, you don't just show up one day and become a CEO, astronaut, or gold medalist. As a general rule, it takes a lot of effort, planning, and grunt work to be exceptional at ANYTHING. Even if you just want to be a great father or the best friend you can be to another human being, it helps a lot to know that's what you're trying to do.

That's because it's very rare that anyone is "accidentally" great at anything over the long haul. People get good at things because they have figured out it's important to be good at them and then they take steps to improve.

The Power of Your Mind

4. **Winners take responsibility for their own lives while losers point the finger elsewhere:** It's not society's job, Wall Street's job or the government's job to take care of you. That's YOUR JOB. David took the responsibility upon himself even though he was not in the military.

Winners take responsibility for what happens to them, their own lives, and their future. That gives them a sense of control over their own destiny. It also puts the onus for change on the shoulders of the only person who has any sort of realistic chance to make a difference: YOU!

On the other hand, losers evade responsibility and point the finger elsewhere when they fail — which is a huge mistake because it cedes control of their own life to other parties. If you're waiting for "society" or the "government" to show up, fix all your problems, and make you into a success, you're going to be in for a long, long wait.

5. **Winners work harder than losers:** What people often think of as natural talent is really the result of a freakish amount of Put in 10,000 hours of well-coached focused practice and you, too, can appear to have an extraordinary amount of "talent." There's a lot to this way of thinking.

Although hard work alone isn't sufficient to make you into a winner, it's a prerequisite for being a winner. That's why successful people are almost inevitably busy people. Long story short: You're never going to become a champion at anything working 40 hours a week and then spending the rest of the week watching TV and playing Xbox.

Problems your shortcut to prominence

6. **Winners fail more often than losers:** The loser tastes defeat and quits. The winner gets knocked down and keeps on getting back up.

> *I've missed more than 9000 shots in my career. I've lost almost 300 games. 26 times, I've been trusted to take the game winning shot and missed. I've failed over and over and over again in my life. And that is why I succeed.*
> MICHAEL JORDAN

Winners have "been there, done that, and got the t-shirt" — so when they're in that same situation again, they've learned from hard experience what to do and what not to do. Losers, on the other hand, fail, decide it's too hard, and they quit before they've ever really gotten started.

7. **Winners ask. Losers wait to be asked:**

> *...Perhaps only 45% of success is showing up, while another 45% of success is asking. Asking is the simplest, most efficient, and potentially most rewarding action a person can take. I've become such a believer in the power of asking that I am compelled to share with you my Ten Sacred Rules of Success: Rule No. 1: Ask Rule No. 2: Ask again. Rule No. 3: Ask again. Rule No. 4: Ask again. Rule No. 5: Ask again. Rule No. 6: Ask again. Rule No. 7: Ask again. Rule No. 8: Ask again. Rule No. 9: Ask again. Rule No. 10: Ask again.*
> ROBERT RINGER

Everybody loves the idea of having someone show up, recognize his obvious merit, and then hand him success on a silver platter. Yet usually, that's not how it happens. If you want good things in your life, you need to have the merit, be the one who shows up and be the one who asks for it. More often than not, you'll hear a "no," but over time the "yesses" will accumulate and make a big difference in your life.

GOLIATH WAS DAVID'S STEPPING STONE TO PROMINENCE

One should never impose one's views on a problem; one should rather study it, and in time a solution will reveal itself.
ALBERT EINSTEIN

Cultivate burning desire to solve the problem you face. Visualize inspiring and joyful problem-free future. Analyze the problem for a short time, brainstorm some solutions but don't finalize any. What you need to do is just to start the ball rolling, and then let your subconscious mind take over the task. Saturate yourself in the problem and then take a break. Shelve the problem for a day or two, even if you think you can already see a solution. Don't think about it — it should not weigh on your conscious mind.

Although you are not consciously thinking about the problem, your subconscious is working on it and will amaze you by a simple and elegant solution that is nearly impossible to produce deliberately using a linear, logical thought process.

It's obvious that what David had and the others in that nation lacked was a different mindset. They were faced with the same problem but they approached it differently. They saw it differently. And the man with the winner's mindset came up with the solution. But it didn't stop there. That problem became his shortcut to prominence.

In 1 Samuel 18:1-8, David had moved from being a shepherd boy to the head of the army in Israel without any military experience. The women in the land also sang his praise — *"Saul has slain his thousands, And David his ten thousand."*

He moved from being a shepherd boy in the wilderness in just a day to being compared with the king of one of the greatest nation on earth at that time, thanks to the problem he solved. Goliath became his stepping stone out of a life of mediocrity.

David and Goliath's story has helped us to understand that though the problem might be complex, the solution is not always far-fetched. This ability to come up with solutions to complex problems has been and will always be the difference between humans and animals. And the key to unlocking this solution is locked up in your mind.

Just as an athlete with go to the gym to exercise his muscles for strength so also should you question your mind always, task your mind, think and come up with solutions. This activity of questioning your mind and thinking is your psychological gym and it will amaze you the solutions you will come up with when a problem arise.

NUGGETS

- Humans have gained more of an advantage over animals simply because humans have a mind and have put it to work.

- People who use their mind have become prominent and those that refuse to use their mind have remained mediocre.

- The people who are not learning to task their mind to proffer solutions are falling behind. The nations who are not bothered about coming up with solutions to their problems are also falling behind.

- There is power in your mind to solve any, I mean any problem.

- New problems will emerge every now and then. And the old solution might be obsolete. Therefore, you need to prepare your mind to always think outside the box. Your mind must be prepared to always think solutions and answers.

- Having a mind that can expand its reality or context quickly is an important form of leverage.

- The first thing to do when you see a problem is to question your mind. The *'Problem'* is not really the problem.

Problems Your Shortcut to Prominence

- Fear is a thing of the mind. Instead of responding to problems with fear, train your mind to think of solutions when a problem arises.

- If you're waiting for "society" or the "government" to show up, fix all your problems, and make you into a success, you're going to be in for a long, long wait.

CHAPTER 10

EXPAND YOUR CAPACITY TO SOLVE PROBLEMS

Congratulations on making it thus far in this book. If you are still here, then you are the real deal. It shows you are ready to expand your capacity to crush any problem or challenge that want to stand between you and your prominence.

Having read numerous examples of people who have harnessed the potential in their minds to influence their world and the way we lead our lives today, it is also very important that you guard your heart against negativity. Definitely, the negative thoughts, pessimistic ideas, the survival mentality will keep throwing itself at you. Nevertheless, it's left to you to choose between prominence and mediocrity. As you already know that your shortcut to prominence is a factor of the problems you solve.

> *Negative thoughts are like birds — they will be always flying over your head but do not let them build a nest in your mind and heart.*
> FOLK WISDOM

These beliefs might have originated from your childhood, perhaps you were told by someone you respect that prominence and greatness is unreal for you and having drawn negative conclusions from your previous experiences, you have convinced yourself that success is unreal without money and connections, which you do not have, so it means that you are not meant to be great.

Unfortunately, this distorted mindset puts obstacles in the way of your greatness and blocks your view from seeing possible solutions. These negative thoughts steal your energy and arouse unnecessary emotions inside you.

You should alter your restricted vision in order to become capable of making headway. A man becomes what he thinks about. Your thoughts will eventually become your reality.

Ordinary people think about their problems and they always complain and object to something; doing so they assign doom to themselves because this is how the law of defeat works.

All a problem is telling you is that something is not currently working and that you need to find a new way around it. Therefore,

Decide to concentrate on the solutions to problems.

Decide to never think of fears.

Decide to never think of doubts.

Don't be afraid of anything, ever.

Finally, think and act.

EXPAND YOUR CAPACITY TO SOLVE PROBLEMS

IGNORE THE NAY-SAYERS

When the Wright brothers announced that they were going to be the first humans to fly, many people said, 'Humans can never fly.' In fact, one of the people who said that was their own father, a respected man of the church."

The reason so many people said, "Humans will never fly," was because that idea was outside the border of the known reality of most people at that time. But that idea was not outside the realm of possibility for the Wright brothers, and they spent years working on making the possibility a reality.

When it comes to problems, that is the same thing great men and women did and the ordinary men failed to do. Today, the common phrase is, "Be willing to think outside the box." But everyone can think outside the box for a few hours or a day. The question is, can you think outside the box for years? Can you think outside the box when you encounter any problem? Can you make it your habit? Can you apply this principle to every problem? If you can, you will become prominent.

The lesson is that your mind is your most powerful tool to solve any problem. Whatever you think is real becomes reality, in most cases. A person who thinks solving national problems is impractical will often find all the reality they want to substantiate that reality. This person will open the newspaper and read about all the problems and how many people have tried solving it in the past that were not successful. In other words, the mind has the power to see whatever it thinks is real and blind itself to any other reality.

Problems Your Shortcut to Prominence

Just as people including their father said to the Wright brothers, "humans will never fly," and to Christopher Columbus, "Can't you see the world is flat?" People will always have their own realities.

In order to be an expert at solving problems and secure your place in history, one of the most important things you can learn to do is to take control of your own reality. If you can learn to do that, becoming prominent will become easy. If you cannot control and change your reality, then you are certainly not ready for a life of success.

> *One of the lessons that I grew up with was to always stay true to yourself and never let what somebody else says distract you from your goals. And so when I hear about negative and false attacks, I really don't invest any energy in them, because I know who I am.*
>
> MICHELLE OBAMA

Ignore statements such as:

- "I tried that once and it did not work."
- "That's impossible. It will never work."
- "You can't do that."
- "That's too hard to do."
- "No one has ever done that before."

Instead ask yourself, "How can I do it?" or "How can I improve on this?" or "How can I learn it?"

TAKE ACTION

"Well, if I talked a lot I should be like a parrot, which is the bird that speaks most and flies least."

Wilbur Wright, who made this quip, was a doer, not a talker. It's not enough to say it or disagree with the status quo, go ahead and do something about it. Be proactive.

At an early flight demonstration, one observer wrote:

Wilbur Wright is the best example of the strength of character that I have ever seen. In spite of the sarcastic remarks and mockery, in spite of the traps set up from everywhere all these years, he has not faltered. He is sure of himself, of his genius, and he kept his secret. He had the desire to participate today to prove the world he had not lied.

When they were just getting started, the brothers were able to shut out the rest of the world and focus on their work. Kitty Hawk turned out to be an excellent place for allowing them to do that. Years later, when they finally attained great wealth and fame, both brothers remembered those simple days at Kitty Hawk as the happiest time of their lives.

"The best dividends on the labor invested have invariably come from seeking more knowledge rather than more power."

This quote from Wilbur provides an interesting insight into their development of some of the earliest planes. Each new model often came with more powerful motors, but that wasn't where the big improvements came from. Instead, discovering an improved "scientific design" resulted in better planes.

Problems Your Shortcut to Prominence

I think this quote is a nice illustration of the principle of working smarter. Sometimes, we're tempted to just apply more muscle to a project or a problem. Stopping to learn and think about how we might improve the process can often yield even greater results.

"The man who wishes to keep at the problem long enough to really learn anything positively must not take dangerous risks. Carelessness and overconfidence are usually more dangerous than deliberately accepted risks."

Wilbur recognized early on one of the key dilemmas facing early flight enthusiasts. One needed a lot of experience in order to master the various difficulties involved, yet each "experiment" could possibly result in death or serious injury.

The brothers were able to solve this problem by being disciplined about managing risks during their early flights. First, they made sure they didn't go too high up. And they, of course, practiced on the beach at Kitty Hawk, N.C., so there was soft sand on which to land. As a result of their precautions, they were able to log countless hours in the sky, which was one of the main reasons they achieved their breakthrough. Like a lot of great investors, they were prudent, but not overly cautious, in their approach to risk-taking.

The early pioneers of flight faced tremendous obstacles. The experiments were expensive and extremely dangerous. And those brave souls who devoted themselves to developing "flying machines" were ridiculed as cranks and fools.

Expand Your Capacity to Solve Problems

Such knowledge makes the achievements of the Wright Brothers all the more remarkable.

In no way did any of this discourage or deter Wilbur and Orville Wright, any more than the fact they had no college education, no formal technical training, no experience working with anyone other than themselves, no friends in high places, no financial backers, no government subsidies, and little money of their own.

Instead, the brothers remained focused on their mission with an unyielding determination. Learning how to fly is one of the greatest accomplishments in all of human history. The incredible discipline, determination, and courage of the Wright brothers is a lesson for you and me. I truly believe that each of us can improve ourselves greatly by learning from their remarkable example.

You can solve any problem, overcome any obstacle or achieve any goal that you can set for yourself by using your wonderful creative mind and then taking action consistently and persistently until you attain your objective.

INVEST YOUR TIME

Many of the people you read about in this book and a lot more which space would not permit me to mention became great in their spare time. A lot of them discovered the solution to the problem they were trying to solve in their spare time.

Do you even have an idea how valuable that spare can be to you? Have you ever thought about what you do with your time? Are you spending or investing your time?

Problems your shortcut to prominence

Some only learn the value of time when it's too late!
Stephen Richards

There's a huge difference between spending time and investing it. The word "spending" means that you're using something up or exhausting it. When you spend time, you're not really looking to get anything back.

When you invest in something you expend resources, but you do so with an expectation of getting a good return on your investment (ROI). Investing your time means that you engage in activities which are calculated to bring you meaningful rewards.

"Investing" and "ROI" are terms which, up until now, you've probably heard only when it comes to money. However, you should start thinking of these terms when it comes to your time, as well.

Michael Dell of Dell technologies went from college kid to billionaire in three years. While his classmates were doing their homework or playing around, he was building a billion-dollar business in his dormitory room.

At the age of 15, he purchased an early Apple computer in order to take it apart to see how it worked. In college, he started building computers and selling them directly to people, focusing on strong customer support and cheaper prices. Dell Computer was the world's largest PC maker.

Michael Dell helped launch the personal computer revolution in the 1980s with the creation of the Dell Computer Corporation (now known as Dell Inc.), which began in the

Expand Your Capacity to Solve Problems

founder's dorm room at the University of Texas and quickly blossomed into a megawatt computer company. By 1992, just eight years after Dell was founded, Michael Dell was the youngest CEO of a Fortune 500 company.

Some are wondering how Michael Dell, a college dropout, got so lucky. He simply invested his time. His luck began with a difference in mindset, a willingness to invest his time to study, not necessarily for better grades, and a willingness to work hard at it.

> *Men talk of killing time, while time quietly kills them.*
> DION BOUCICAULT

Are you spending your time watching TV re-runs, or are you investing your time in leisure activities? Are you spending your time sleeping more hours than your body really needs? Are you spending your time complaining about your problems, or are you investing your time in finding a solution?

When your friends play golf or go fishing or watch sports on TV, you can be starting your part-time business. This time can be converted into added value. Invest this time to study, learn new skills, improve on existing skills and be the best at what you do. Exhaust the literature on the problem you are working on.

The likes of Albert Einstein, Bill Gates, Aliko Dangote, Steve Jobs, Michael Dell, and Thomas Edison, all have the same 24 hours, each day as you do. You've got no reason not to be prominent. You don't have an excuse not to be great.

Problems your shortcut to prominence

To expand your capacity for solving problems, you may want to begin by investing your time in reading books or listening to recordings about people who have already achieved what you want to achieve. Reading is a sure way to expand your capacity to solve problems.

HABITS OF PROMINENT INDIVIDUALS

- Prominent individuals concentrate their attention on their tasks while ordinary people think of problems.
- Prominent individuals are constantly thinking about solutions, ways, and methods to solve a certain problem.
- They are always in deep thought about their goal. They are permanently looking for solutions to promote their set goals and tasks.
- They are people of goals, they constantly think of new goals and tasks.
- Prominent people reflect on their future, building their tomorrow today.
- They are constantly thinking.
- Successful people always have a positive vision of life.
- They do not think of defeat. They do not picture something to be impossible.

- They do not take the word "NO" as an answer. They are positively tuned in and they never give up.

- Great people permanently reflect on the improvement of their affairs. They have never been in a state of inactivity. They constantly work on improving themselves and doing everything more efficiently.

- Successful people concentrate their attention on actions.

- Something must be done and it must be done excellently. They cannot forgive their idleness. They do not relax in their actions.

- They constantly question the status quo. They task their minds. They've trained their minds to see solutions or look for solutions to every problem.

- Successful people think about how to do everything better and faster.

- They are always on the lookout for a way to do everything better and faster.

- They value time. They invest their time.

LEARN FROM YOUR FAILURES

Another very important tool that can expand your capacity to solve problems is learning from your failures. Don't let anyone deceive you; you might probably not get it right the first time. But this should not deter you from trying again.

Problems your shortcut to prominence

Thomas Edison the America's great inventor, famous for inventing the light bulb and holding thousands of patents, it was actually one of Edison's early failures that taught him the vital relationship between invention and marketing. In 1869 he patented an Electronic Vote Recorder to tally votes in the Massachusetts state legislature faster and more accurately.

To Edison's astonishment, it flopped. Edison had not taken into account legislators' habits. They don't *like* to vote quickly and efficiently. They *do* like to lobby their fellow legislators to promote their viewpoints as voting takes place. (Not much has changed in 140 years.) In other words, Edison had a great idea, but he completely misunderstood the needs of his potential customers.

But here is the difference between this man and a lot of others. While the first invention flopped, he didn't give up on the idea. He tried again. But this time, he used the lesson he learnt from the failures he had earlier on.

> *You build on failure. You use it as a stepping stone. Close the door on the past. You don't try to forget the mistakes, but you don't dwell on it. You don't let it have any of your energy, or any of your time, or any of your space.*
> **JOHNNY CASH**

Edison realized that marketing and invention must be joined at the hip. "Anything that won't sell, I don't want to invent," he said. "Its sale is proof of utility, and utility is success." He realized he needed to put the customers' needs first and tailor his thinking accordingly, despite any temptation to invent for invention's sake. This mindset paved the way for tremendous marketing success. The six industries (and their offshoots) Edison pioneered between 1873 and 1905 are estimated to be worth more than $1 trillion today.

IMPROVE ON THE EXISTING SOLUTION

> *A man must be big enough to admit his mistakes, smart enough to profit from them, and strong enough to correct them.*
> JOHN C. MAXWELL

In putting customers' needs first, Edison became one of the world's earliest market researchers. He literally went to homes and places of work to analyze how people struggled in order to gain the insight he needed to invent products that could help them do it better, faster and more efficiently. He looked first for unmet needs and then applied science and creativity to fill them.

Here in lies the secret to every problem you want to solve. You have to do your homework. Research thoroughly on the topic under question. There is never an end to solving problems. There is no dead end to success. Keep improving. Keep innovating. Seek for better ways to get things done and you will be amazed how your capacity to solve problems will expand.

The first example of Edison's success using a "needs-first" approach to the invention is one we seldom associate with him: Document duplication. The inkling of pursuing invention work in the insurance industry came to him while reading post-Civil War newspaper articles documenting the re-building of the South, and the tremendous demand it created for insurance policies.

Edison got permission from insurance agents to watch their clerks at work. He saw that most of their day was spent hand-copying documents for each party to the insurance sale instead of selling insurance. Edison realized that if he could invent something that would save both the insurance clerks and agents' time writing, they could all make more money. And who doesn't like to make more money?

> *Strive for perfection in everything you do.*
> *Take the best that exists and make it better.*
> *When it does not exist, design it.*
> FAD IBRA

Edison's first solution was the Edison Electric Pen and Press. Introduced in 1873, it could make as many as 5,000 copies of a single document. A few years later, his second-generation solution superseded the first by bringing a more automated process into play: The Edison Mimeograph Machine. He sold the patent for the mimeograph to the A.B. Dick Company, providing Edison money to invest in his new laboratory at Menlo Park, New Jersey.

The mimeograph machine is familiar to anyone over age 40 who remembers that mysteriously addicting smell emanating from the Principal's office, where hundreds of take-home math worksheets were printed using funky purple ink.

EXPAND YOUR CAPACITY TO SOLVE PROBLEMS

> *You don't learn from successes; you don't learn from awards; you don't learn from a celebrity; you only learn from wounds and scars and mistakes and failures. And that's the truth.*
>
> JANE FONDA

Thomas Edison, inventor of the light bulb, the phonograph, the storage battery and moving pictures, applied this principle to solve all these problems. Beyond his mastery of bringing inspiration, perseverance and mental acuity to his work, he believed in the power of practical, honest market research to spur product innovation. And he put customer needs first rather than simply invent for invention's sake.

It's not enough to just go out there and think you have to solve problems for solving sake. There is a lot more to that. Do your research, study and come up with a solution that will impact and influence the world at large.

In case you need more light on how to better resolve issues and become an expert in resolving problems, the next chapter will do justice to that. And I'm pretty sure since you've gone this far, you don't want to leave any page unturned. I'm certain you wouldn't want to miss out on any of the secrets to prominence contained in the next chapter.

NUGGETS

- A man becomes what he thinks about. Your thoughts will eventually become your reality.

- Ordinary people think about their problems and they always complain and object to something; doing so they assign doom to themselves because this is how the law of defeat works.

- All a problem is telling you is that something is not currently working and that you need to find a new way around it.

- Everyone can think outside the box for a few hours or a day. The question is, can you think outside the box for years? Can you make it your habit? Can you apply this principle to every problem? If you can, you will become prominent.

- Your mind is your most powerful tool to solve any problem.

- The likes of Albert Einstein, Bill Gates, Aliko Dangote, Steve Jobs, Michael Dell, and Thomas Edison, all have the same 24 hours, each day as you do. You've got no reason not to be prominent. You don't have an excuse not to be great.

- To expand your capacity for solving problems, you may want to begin by investing your time in reading books or listening to recordings

Expand Your Capacity to Solve Problems

about people who have already achieved what you want to achieve. Reading is a sure way to expand your capacity to solve problems.

CHAPTER 11

IT'S NEVER TOO LATE!

When I run into people who say, "I'm too old," I ask them if they would be willing to read the story of Colonel Sanders, a man who did not become prominent until he was in his sixties. When I hear a woman say, "I can't get ahead because it's a man's world," I ask her if she has read the story of Coco Chanel, founder of House of Chanel.

When people say they are too young, I ask them to read about Bill Gates, a person who became the richest man in the world in his early thirties; or Mark Zuckerberg, the founder of Facebook; or King David in the Bible, who defeated Goliath — a giant that posed the greatest problem to the nation of Israel.

And maybe Joseph will be the best example for you, a man who saved the economy of a nation at a very young age from prison and this promoted him to the second in-command in Egypt. If those stories do not expand your mind and what you think is possible, I doubt if anything will.

WHAT IS YOUR EXCUSE?

I believe the purpose of your life is to find and do the purpose of your life — your truest passions. For me, it's writing self-help books and raising leaders that transform

Problems Your Shortcut to Prominence

nations. For others, it's creating new technology, designing various products, learning medicine — and at least one person was put on this planet to invent that little plastic doohickey which holds up the pizza box.

I recognize there are many challenges on your path to greatness, and you can often grow discouraged. But far too often it's not outside circumstances which stop you — but your internal beliefs. Far too many people get in their own way of greatness — by telling themselves what I call "Blame Excuses" and "Myth taken Thinking."

For example, right now you might be telling yourself you're too old, too broke, too inexperienced to snag your passions. If so, let me tell you about a guy named Colonel Harland Sanders.

When the Colonel first tried to sell his chicken recipe he was 65 years old — with only a small pension — a tiny bit of money in the bank — and an old Caddie roadster. His first plan was to sell his chicken recipe to restaurant owners, who'd give him a residual for every chicken piece sold — a nickle per chicken.

He knocked on the first restaurateur's door and was greeted by a NOPE. Second door: NOPE. Third door: NOPE. In fact, his first 1008 sales call all served up a NOPE. Still, the Colonel continued to call on owners as he traveled across the USA, sleeping in his Caddie to save money.

It wasn't until prospect number 1,009 that the Colonel received his first YES. Then, after two years of making daily sales, he had only signed up a total of five restaurants. Still, the Colonel kept knocking on doors, staying passionately

It's Never Too Late!

focused in the belief that his golden fried chicken would create a big pile of gold.

Finally, by 1963, the Colonel procured 600 restaurants across the country to sell his Kentucky Fried Chicken (KFC)! In 1964 he was bought out by a multi-millionaire — who made The Colonel a multi-millionaire himself.

I love this story — because it's an "against all odds" tale. The Colonel was a senior citizen, with no money, entering a new field — and yet he succeeded! How? He knew how to fuel his greatness instead of fueling his fears, insecurity, and excuses. Robert Louis Stevenson said it well when he said:

"To know what you prefer, instead of humbly saying amen to what the world tells you that you ought to prefer, is to have kept your soul alive."

LESSONS FROM COLONEL SANDERS

Colonel Sanders was rejected 1009 times before successfully selling his Kentucky Fried Chicken recipe. He had failed at every job he'd tried earlier on in his life, lawyer, salesman, you name it.

The Colonel was already married at the young age of 19 to his wife Josephine, had 3 children, then had frequent affairs and the marriage ended in divorce. It's safe to say that he didn't have the best of lives growing up. In fact, he didn't even successfully sell his company until he was 75 years old!

There's no doubt that the odds were stacked against the KFC king. The Colonel's story is so inspiring and filled with hope for others who think it's too late.

Check out some of the most powerful success lessons we can all learn from Colonel Sanders. It doesn't matter whether you're 20 years old or 70.

YOU HAVE TO GO THROUGH FAILURE TO GET TO SUCCESS

In the intro above, I mentioned that Colonel Sanders was rejected more than 1000 times before successfully selling his KFC recipe.

...1000 TIMES!

Not only that, but I also mentioned that he'd failed at every other career he'd tried to get into. Sanders tried and failed miserably at all the below careers between the ages of 10 and 40:

- Farming
- Streetcar Conductor
- Lawyer
- Insurance Salesman
- Railroad Fireman

Just goes to show that no matter how many failures you experience in life, there's always still time to be successful. For anyone reading this who thinks it's too late to make something of your life, start re-thinking!

YOU'RE NEVER TOO OLD TO SUCCEED

Colonel Sanders was 75 years old before he finally sold Kentucky Fried Chicken for a cool $2 million, which would be around about $15 million in the world of today. He remained as the spokesmen for the company after the sale.

But 75 years old... the majority of people, at least 95% give up way earlier in life. People stop thinking they can be successful even in their 30's! And yet, the Colonel didn't think this way and ended up being the founder and face of a billion dollar brand.

So before you start to think that you can't achieve your dreams, before you start nursing those thoughts that you can't be of any significance because you're 30, 40, 50 years old... stop. You're never too old to achieve success in life. There is no age grade for prominence. You're never too old to provide solutions.

THE PAST DOESN'T DEFINE YOUR SUCCESS

An awesome success lesson that many people need to hear, is the lesson that your past doesn't define your future success. It doesn't matter how many times you've failed. It doesn't matter where you were brought up, or what happened to you earlier on in life.

Your past does not determine how successful you can become in the future.

Again, look at Sanders. He'd failed at every other career he'd tried... a whole bunch of them! He was in an unhappy marriage and had 3 children at a very young age. For most people, that's when they start to quit on life, and can't see a way out.

GIVING UP IS THE ONLY SURE WAY TO FAIL

You can fail at a lot of things in life, but the KFC story proves that giving up is the only sure way to fail. If you're some like the Colonel, no matter how many times you fail, the possibility of success is still always on the table.

You're not a failure until you finally stop trying.

So don't give up. Even if time is passing, you're slowly getting older and you still can't quite see the end of the tunnel. It's never impossible to achieve success.

IT'S NEVER TOO LATE TO START OVER

It was clear that cooking was the Colonel's passion, but it wasn't discovered by himself until later on in his life. He went through a complete range of careers, having to start over from scratch, again, and again.

> *Follow your passion. The rest will attend to itself. If I can do it, anybody can do it. It's possible. And it's your turn. So go for it. It's never too late to become what you always wanted to be in the first place.*
> J. MICHAEL STRACZYNSKI

When you try to succeed at so many different things, it can become exhausting. The start is always the hardest part, and for most people starting all over again at the age of 50, or 60 would be unthinkable. Yet, it's never too late, and Colonel Sanders showed this by finally being successful at doing what he loved... in his 70's! Find what you are passionate about and take action on it.

DON'T BE AFRAID TO START SMALL

Sanders started selling Kentucky Fried Chicken by the side of the road, on a small scale. After selling the recipe, it vastly grew, and franchises were being opened all over the world. The lesson here is not to be afraid to start small. As long as you get started, and work hard, progression will come.

> *"Hard work beats all the tonics and vitamins in the world."*
> COLONEL SANDERS

People often put off starting their own business, website, Non-Governmental Organizations (NGOs) and such, simply because they don't think it's at a big enough scale to launch. I see plenty of people in the process of websites or NGOs, stuck in this process for more than 2 years because they don't think it's quite ready.

JUST START! SERIOUSLY!

People love progression, and once you start you'll be able to do so. Putting things off because of perfection is not going to get you anywhere.

Just to recap on these awesome lessons we can all learn from Colonel Sanders, and the story of KFC:

1. You have to go through failure to get to success
2. You're never too old to succeed
3. The past doesn't define your success
4. Your past does not determine how successful you can become in the future
5. Giving up is the only sure way to fail
6. You are not a failure until you stop trying
7. It's never too late to start over
8. Don't be afraid to start small

If there's any one point you could take away from this; for me it would be the fact that it's never too late, and you're never too old, to go after your dreams or what you are passionate about because that is a pointer to the problem you are here to solve.

I won't stop here; I'll also like to tell you the story of Coco Chanel especially for the women. Nevertheless, I know that you can still take something away from this as a man.

THE WOMAN WHO CHANGED THE WORLD OF FASHION

Coco Chanel successfully immortalized herself in the world of fashion. She started a beauty line and up till now, she is still prominent. Why? She was promoted to prominence by the problem she resolved. She is long dead but she is ever remembered.

Coco Chanel (1883–1971) is an outstanding French fashion designer, creator of the fashion empire of the 20th century. She is the founder of The House of Chanel. Her net worth is $15 billion. Her real name is Gabrielle Chanel.

> *Fashion is what one wears oneself. What is unfashionable is what other people wear.*
> COCO CHANEL

This is the famous quotation from Oscar Wilde. It was disproved by Coco Chanel in the mid-20s of the previous century who stated that fashion was the *"little black dress"*. Her authority was so great that women from different social classes unhesitatingly were wearing Chanel clothing.

EARLY LIFE

Coco was born on August 19, 1883, in Saumur, France in the family of fair trader Albert Chanel and his girlfriend Eugénie Jeanne Devolle. He married Jeanne Devolle several years after Coco Chanel was born. They did not have a permanent place to live. If things went well, they allowed themselves to have a primitive farm and settled down in some old abandoned shack, which people tried to get round.

The legendary Mademoiselle Chanel had been shy of her miserable childhood all her life. She was afraid that reporters could find out about her extramarital origins, her mother's death from bronchitis at the age of 31 or about her father who simply gave up having passed Coco in a shelter at the age of 12.

Coco Chanel even invented her story that when her mother died, her father sailed for America, and she lived in a cozy and clean house with two strict aunts, who in reality did not exist.

> *If you were born without wings, do nothing to prevent them from growing.*
> Coco Chanel

WHAT WOULD YOU DO, IF THE ODDS WERE STACKED AGAINST YOU?

Having learned sewing arts during her six years at Aubazine shelter, Coco Chanel was able to find a job as a seamstress. When not plying her trade with a needle and thread, she was singing in a cabaret "La Rotonde" frequented by cavalry officers. There she acquired her nickname "Coco" (real name — Gabrielle). It is derived from the famous song "Qui Qu'a Vu Coco?" that she used to sing.

In 1910, Coco became a licensed modiste (hat maker) and opened a boutique named *Chanel Modes* on 21 Rue Cambon in Paris. Soon the street became known throughout the world and had been linked to her name for half a century.

In 1913, Coco Chanel opened her boutique in Deauville that quickly attracted regular clients. The creator of the famous hats dreamt of developing her own line of women's clothing. At this time, she had no right to make a 'real' woman's dresses, as she could be brought to justice for illegal competition because she was not a licensed dressmaker.

It's Never Too Late!

Coco found the solution. She started sewing dresses of jersey fabric, which had been only used for men's underwear and earned her first capital on it.

Notice here that she did not complain or blame the authorities for not been a licensed dressmaker. What did she do? She found a solution to the problem. She thought outside the box and came up with something no one else has ever done. She invented something new entirely.

What do you do when faced with obstacles? How to you react to situations like this? Do you run away from there? Or you look for a solution to the problem?

CONSTANTLY GENERATE NEW IDEAS

All of her dress-discoveries were born that way. Chanel quickly became the world fashion designer, turning over the spotlight. She created a style that had been previously unthinkable for women — tracksuits. The style produced by The House of Chanel was simple, practical and elegant.

Coco continued to work vigorously, presenting new demands for clothing and generating new ideas: the first female skinny suit from Chanel. A couple of years later, she sewed a redingote without a belt and ornaments, removing the bust and curves with almost masculine stringency. She created an understated waist, dress shirt, pants for women and beach pajamas.

> *In order to be irreplaceable, one must always be different.*
> Coco Chanel

THE BIRTH OF CHANEL NO. 5 PERFUME

It was the first synthetic perfume of eighty components that were not repeating the smell of a particular flower, as it had been earlier. Designers spilled the golden liquid into a crystal bottle with a modest rectangular label that looked to them a peculiar solution; usually, perfume bottles had intricate shapes.

As a result, the world had a 'perfume for women that smelt like a woman'. The success experienced its creators — Chanel No. 5 is still the best-selling perfume in the world. As of 2014, the revenue of Chanel reached $7.43 billion.

The marketing policy of The House of Chanel was targeted to celebrities. This choice was not accidental: in the list of clients who wore Chanel No. 5 perfume were the most beautiful women of the century. Chanel No. 5 was a favorite perfume of Jacqueline Kennedy.

However unwittingly, Marilyn Monroe invaluably promoted "Chanel". Moreover, she did it free. In the early 1950s, in one of the interviews, Marilyn said that all she wore in bed was a few drops of Chanel No. 5 perfume. A few days later her statement skyrocketed sales of Chanel No. 5 perfume.

THE LITTLE BLACK DRESS

By the early 20s, the world almost ended up in fighting for gender inequality. Fashion was going through a situation where due to the sad egalitarianism women's clothing began to lose its sexiness and sophistication.

It's Never Too Late!

Coco Chanel got this point and successfully managed to combine incredible details in her models with revolutionary innovations and defiant femininity. She invented the famous "little black dress", which seemed, at first, glance, artless, rustic garb and impersonal. This decisive step brought the designer worldwide fame and made her finding a symbol of elegance, luxury, and good taste.

After World War II, designers appeared like mushrooms after the rain in postwar France. One of them, a young fashion designer Christian Dior commented about Coco Chanel's design: *"With a black pullover and ten rows of pearls she revolutionized fashion."*

Americans gave her an ovation. There was a triumph of the little black dress in the United States. It was an honor to a new generation of fashionable women to wear Chanel clothes and Coco herself turned into a tycoon, managing the largest fashion house in the world fashion industry.

During these years, she created the *Pink Chanel* suit. On November 22, 1963, when the President John F. Kennedy was assassinated his wife wore a double-breasted, strawberry pink and navy trim collared Chanel wool suit.

In the 1960s, the *Pink Chanel* suit has become a symbol for her husband's assassination and one of the iconic items of fashion. Many times the suit has been shamelessly copied to the last braid, to the last golden button and stitching. Nevertheless, the name of Coco Chanel is more than a suit.

Coco Chanel once said: *"Fashion fades; only style remains the same."*

Problems your shortcut to prominence

The world has recognized her as the only trendsetter of the most refined elegance. The Chanel's style concept firmly anchored in the fashion industry. The Chanel's style means that a suit should be functional and comfortable. If a Chanel suit has buttons, they certainly should be buttoned. By the way, the idea of wearing a bag over shoulder also belongs to Mademoiselle Coco.

You who is reading this now, I want you to know that as an individual, you are here to solve problems. You are here to make the world a better place. It is not a mistake that you are here. You are not an afterthought.

I took my time to narrate to you a little about their background so you know that they are ordinary individuals like you. Maybe, your story might be better than theirs? Maybe, this is just what you need to get you up and running?

And no greater joy can I experience than to see you get up on your feet dishing out that solution that is inside of you for the improvement and development of this world. Do not resign to fate and inactivity in the guise that the problems or obstacles are too much for you alone to handle.

Get up on your feet right now, throw out all the excuses, stop existing and start living!

NUGGETS

- No matter how many failures you experience in life, there's always still time to be successful.

- Before you start nursing those thoughts that you can't be of any significance because you're 30, 40, 50 years old… stop. You're never too old to achieve success in life. There is no age grade for prominence. You're never too old to provide solutions.

- Your past doesn't define your future success. It doesn't matter how many times you've failed. It doesn't matter where you were brought up, or what happened to you earlier on in life.

- The start is always the hardest part, and for most people starting all over again at the age of 50, or 60 would be unthinkable. Yet, it's never too late, and Colonel Sanders showed this by finally being successful at doing what he loved… in his 70's! Find what you are passionate about and take action on it.

- Do not resign to fate and inactivity in the guise that the problems or obstacles are too much for you alone to handle.

CHAPTER 12

STOP EXISTING, START LIVING!

What problem have you decided to dedicate your life to resolve? What are the issues you have decided to dedicate your life to? What are the problems you have decided to take head on? What are you going to be prominent for? What are you going to resolve with your life?

That problem will become your shortcut to prominence. That problem that you have decided to resolve is what will cement your name in time and eternity. That problem that you have decided to resolve is what will make you to be remembered long after you are gone. That problem that you have dedicated your life to resolving is what will become your monument.

Prominence is as a result of problem solved. Significance is as a result of the problem solved. Fame is as a result of the problem solved. Problems, therefore are your shortcut to prominence.

In closing, I'll like to remind you once more that you are not needed here on earth if you are not going to solve any problem. You are not needed if you are not going to resolve any issue for which you are made. You are not needed if the world will not become a better place because you came.

JUST ONE!

The time God has given you, what is the result it's going to produce? What answer will the world celebrate you for? At least one issue! Just one! What one issue will you resolve with your life? A whole lifetime, what one issue will it tackle? What problem is your life and all your experiences going to resolve?

What questions will your gifts and talents be directed to answer? What will the end result of all your certificates, masters, Ph.D., name them, be at the end of the day? What result will all your certificates produce? What is the end result of your life?

You will recall that:

Joseph became prominent because he saved a whole nation from famine.

David became prominent because he killed Goliath.

Jesus became prominent because He came to extend God's kingdom on earth.

Thomas Edison became prominent because the electric bulb can now last long hours.

Bill Gates became prominent because of personal computers.

George Washington Carver became prominent because he saved the economy of Southern America post-slavery era.

Malala became prominent because she fought for girl-child education.

Nelson Mandela became prominent because he fought injustice and apartheid.

Rosa Parks became prominent because she fought injustice by refusing to give up her seat on a public bus because of her skin color.

Harriet Tubman became prominent because she saved herself and other slaves. She was the 'Moses' of her time.

Singapore became prominent among other nations in the world because she solved her own problems.

Come on dear friend, what one issue will you resolve with your life? At least one issue! Just one!

These were not the people who had the survival mentality. No! They solved problems. They made the world a better place. They secured their place in history. They built monuments for themselves through the problems they solved. They were the good news to their generation and even to the many that came after them. They had their own share of challenges but they focused on the solution. Little wonder they are prominent today.

THEY HAD THEIR OWN SHARE OF CHALLENGES

Little minds are tamed and subdued by misfortune, but great minds rise above them.
WASHINGTON IRVING

Problems your shortcut to prominence

Every prominent individual you've seen or heard of have had their own share of challenges. They've had issues they had to deal with. But that did not stop them. They were fearless in the face of these challenges. They never gave up.

Walt Disney was fired by a newspaper editor because "he lacked imagination and had no good ideas." He went bankrupt several times before he built Disneyland. In fact, the proposed park was rejected by the city of Anaheim on the grounds that it would only attract riffraff.

Henry Ford failed and went broke five times before he succeeded.

Robert Sternberg received a 'C' in his first college introductory-psychology class. His teacher commented that "there was a famous Sternberg in psychology and it was obvious there would not be another." Three years later Sternberg graduated with honors from Stanford University with exceptional distinction in psychology, *summa cum laude*, and Phi Beta Kappa. In 2002, he became President of the American Psychological Association.

Thomas Edison's teachers said he was "too stupid to learn anything." He was fired from his first two jobs for being "non-productive." As an inventor, Edison made 1,000 unsuccessful attempts at inventing the light bulb. When a reporter asked, "How did it feel to fail 1,000 times?" Edison replied, "I didn't fail 1,000 times. The light bulb was an invention with 1,000 steps."

Charles Darwin gave up a medical career and was told by his father, "You care for nothing but shooting, dogs, and rat catching." In his autobiography, Darwin wrote, "I was considered by all my masters and my father, a very ordinary boy, rather below the common standard of intellect." Clearly, he evolved.

Louis Pasteur was only a mediocre pupil in undergraduate studies and ranked 15th out of 22 students in chemistry. In 1872, Pierre Pachet, Professor of Physiology at Toulouse, wrote that "Louis Pasteur's theory of germs is ridiculous fiction."

Fred Smith, the founder of Federal Express, received a 'C' on his college paper detailing his idea for a reliable overnight delivery service. His professor at Yale told him, "Well, Fred, the concept is interesting and well formed, but in order to earn better than a 'C' grade, your ideas also have to be feasible.

"So we went to Atari and said, 'Hey, we've got this amazing thing, even built with some of your parts, and what do you think about funding us? Or we'll give it to you. We just want to do it. Pay our salary; we'll come work for you.' And they said, 'No.' So, then we went to Hewlett-Packard (HP), and they said, 'Hey, we don't need you. You haven't got through college yet.'" This is the story of Apple Computer founder Steve Jobs on attempts to get Atari and HP interested in his and Steve Wozniak's personal computer.

Michael Jordan couldn't make it to his high school basketball team. Jordan once observed, "I've failed over and over again in my life. That is why I succeed."

Problems your shortcut to prominence

> *I've missed more than 9,000 shots in my career. I've lost almost 300 games 26 times I've been trusted to take the game winning shot... and missed. I've failed over and over and over again in my life. That is why I succeed.*
> — MICHAEL JORDAN

Beethoven handled the violin awkwardly and preferred playing his own compositions instead of improving his technique. His teacher called him "hopeless as a composer." And, of course, you know that he wrote five of his greatest symphonies while completely deaf.

12 publishers rejected J.K. Rowling's book about a boy wizard before a small London house picked up *Harry Potter and the Philosopher's Stone*.

> *No matter how hard you work for success, if your thought is saturated with the fear of failure, it will kill your efforts, neutralize your endeavors and make success impossible.*
> — BAUDJUIN

My dear friend, don't give anything an excuse to stop your greatness. Don't allow personal problems stand in the way of your prominence. There is a greater life. There is a greater assignment. It's the assignment of making the world a better place than you met it. It's the assignment of being a problem solver.

If they had given up in the face of those challenges, this book would have been occupied by other names. They would have been long forgotten.

> *Every great cause is born from repeated*
> *failures and from imperfect achievements.*
> MARIA MONTESSORI

I must confess, I'm not one of those who will tell you that you won't encounter challenges on your way. Truth be told, you will have a lot of them! But they are there for you, not against you because you will learn more from these challenges than any success you achieve.

> *I never learned a thing from*
> *a tournament I won.*
> BOBBY JONES

A COMBINATION OF *LOVE* AND *HATE*

I learned years ago that passion is a combination of love and hate. Unless someone has a passion for something, it is difficult to accomplish anything. Be passionate. Passion gives energy to your life. If you want something you do not have, find out why you love what you want and why you hate not having what you want. When you combine those two thoughts, you will find the energy to get off your seat and go get that problem solved.

So you may want to start with a list comparing loves and hates. For example, I would create the following list and this can be used as a guide:

Problems Your Shortcut to Prominence

LOVE	HATE
Your country	Bad governance
Education for all	Depriving girls their right to education
Entertainment	Piracy or Lack of value in the entertainment industry
Business	Lack of integrity
Politics	Rigging elections

Ask yourself "what can I do to make things different in this sphere? How can I contribute to the improvement of something that is not in best shape here? How can I make things better?" Critically and honestly answering these questions will get your creative minds flowing and I guarantee that ideas will begin to pour in. You may want to start your list of loves and hates in the space below. If you need more space, which I hope you do, find a much larger sheet of paper.

YOUR LOVES	YOUR HATES

COME UP WITH A PLAN

Nobody ever wrote down a plan to be broke, fat, lazy, or stupid. Those things are what happen when you don't have a plan.
LARRY WINGET

For instance, you may not run for political offices, but you have to come up with a plan to influence other aspects of the political system. You might be the one to implement an electoral system that will be truly free and fair across the country. It might be your idea or your NGO that will re-educate the people on the importance of voting and make their votes count without violence. Perhaps, you are the one to develop a program for young people that will teach them how not to allow themselves to be used as political thugs.

You might be the one to get into the business arena in your country and change the way things are done. It might just be a program that you develop that will help create a new breed of businessmen with integrity in the dispensation of their transactions. You might just be the one who is gifted in raising entrepreneurs.

It's just like the story of Nigeria's highest paid blogger, Linda Ikeji. Out of her passion for empowering young ladies and make them stop sleeping with men for money, she started a project for young girls in Nigeria to make them self-made and stop sleeping with men for money.

The idea of the project was for girls to send in their business ideas and face a panel to defend their business ideas. Those chosen will then be financed and funded by Linda herself.

She has chosen the first beneficiaries and given out over 5 million Naira (approximately $20,000) to 15 girls. It doesn't end here as another 5 million Naira is due for another set of girls and Linda wants this to be a yearly project for as long as possible.

While someone is financing their capital to start-up, someone else or another NGO might get involved in teaching them entrepreneurial skills. Imagine if we all come up with solving these little problems in these little ways, How far can we go as a nation? Wouldn't the world be a better place?

In her own words, *"I want to first give away this 10 million Naira ($40,000) and see what the girls do with it before getting others involved. I'm truly hoping to make a new set of self-made women and like I said when it started, I plan to do this for as long as I can."*

Also, Linda said, *"If I see that their business is going well and they are really dedicated and extremely serious about succeeding, I will pump in more money into their businesses and by the end of one year, any lady who has most succeeded with the little they got to set up their business, will get an additional 1 million Naira."*

You also can start up something that will meet a need or two around you. You might just be the next Linda Ikeji that your country needs. You might not be able to fund businesses like she did but you can set up an organization that empowers them with the necessary skills to excel at such businesses. It is a chain of activity. They are all interwoven. It is our call together to make that happen. Therefore, come up with your own plan to solve a problem.

START LIVING!

Imagine you are standing on the bank of one side of the river. A plan is a bridge to your dreams. Your job is to make the plan or bridge real so that your dreams become real and the problem becomes history. If all you do is stand on this side of the bank and dream of the other side, your dreams will forever be just dreams. First, make your plan real, and then the problem will take care of itself. The future we all dream of is created by what you do today, not tomorrow. In other words, what you are doing today is your future.

Make sure that the life you are living on earth or the time you are given to live is an opportunity for you to fill heaven with your own treasure.

Problems Your Shortcut to Prominence

Dedicate your life to something significant. Dedicate your life to something worthwhile. Resolve a problem! Identify something. Take on a problem. Give your life to something. Start living, Stop existing!

Think! Use your mind. Make a difference in your world.

A word is enough for the wise.

Blessings!

NUGGETS

- Prominence is as a result of the problem solved. Significance is as a result of the problem solved. Fame is as a result of the problem solved. Problems, therefore are your shortcut to prominence.

- You are not needed if you are not going to resolve any issue for which you are made. You are not needed if the world will not become a better place because you came.

- The time God has given you, what is the result it's going to produce?

- Every prominent individual you've seen or heard of have had their own share of challenges. They've had issues they had to deal with. But that did not stop them. They were fearless in the face of these challenges.

- I'm not one of those who will tell you that you won't encounter challenges on your way. Truth be told, you will have a lot of them! But they are there for you, not against you because you will learn more from these challenges than any success you achieve.

- If you want something you do not have, find out why you love what you want and why you hate not having what you want. When you combine those two thoughts, you will find the energy to get off your seat and go get that problem solved.

- The future we all dream of is created by what you do today, not tomorrow. In other words, what you are doing today is your future.

FINAL THOUGHTS

Can everyone become prominent? Can you become prominent? I'm sure you have an answer to that question now. Nevertheless, for that to materialize you must put every information you have gathered in this book to good use. The models in every chapter should be your guide.

Over the years, I have come to discover that the only reason why people run away from problems is because they don't want to take responsibility. They don't want to task their mind to come up with solutions.

But if you dare come up and start with the least of problems around you, seeking out ways to solve them, you will be amazed at your life in the nearest future.

> *Everybody can be great...because anybody can serve. You don't have to have a college degree to serve. You don't have to make your subject and verb agree to serve. You only need a heart full of grace. A soul generated by love.*
> MARTIN LUTHER KING JR.

Martin Luther King Jr. is right by telling us anybody can serve. Therefore, serve the world with the solutions God has placed in you. Make the world a better place. You are a problem solver. And this is your shortcut to prominence.

As I close, I'll like to end with this prayer, *"May the world not suffer from the problems you refuse to solve."* Thank you for reading this far. I really can't wait to hear what becomes of you through the application of the wisdom nuggets contained in this book. Feel free to write me anytime, I read every single mail and will be glad to reply you.

pastor@godembassy.org

You can also avail yourself of other training materials of mine on my blog:

www.SundayAdelajaBlog.com

For The Love Of God, Church, And Nation

SUNDAY ADELAJA'S BIOGRAPHY

Pastor Sunday Adelaja is the Founder and Senior Pastor of The Embassy of the Blessed Kingdom of God for All Nations Church in Kyiv, Ukraine.

Sunday Adelaja is a Nigerian-born Leader, Thinker, Philosopher, Transformation Strategist, Pastor, Author and Innovator who lives in Kiev, Ukraine.

At 19, he won a scholarship to study in the former Soviet Union. He completed his master's program in Belorussia State University with distinction in journalism.

At 33, he had built the largest evangelical church in Europe — The Embassy of the Blessed Kingdom of God for All Nations.

Sunday Adelaja is one of the few individuals in our world who has been privileged to speak in the United Nations, Israeli Parliament, Japanese Parliament and the United States Senate.

The movement he pioneered has been instrumental in reshaping lives of people in the Ukraine, Russia and about 50 other nations where he has his branches.

His congregation, which consists of ninety-nine percent white Europeans, is a cross-cultural model of the church for the 21st century.

His life mission is to advance the Kingdom of God on earth by raising a generation of history makers who will live for a cause larger, bigger and greater than themselves. Those who will live like Jesus and transform every sphere of the society in every nation as a model of the Kingdom of God on earth.

His economic empowerment program has succeeded in raising over 200 millionaires in the short period of three years.

Sunday Adelaja is the author of over 300 books, many of which are translated into several languages including Russian, English, French, Chinese, German, etc.

His work has been widely reported by world media outlets such as The Washington Post, The Wall Street Journal, New York Times, Forbes, Associated Press, Reuters, CNN, BBC, German, Dutch and French national television stations.

Pastor Sunday is happily married to his "Princess" Bose Dere-Adelaja. They are blessed with three children: Perez, Zoe and Pearl.

Bill Clinton —
42Nd President Of The United States (1993–2001), Former Arcansas State Governor

Ariel "Arik" Sharon — Israeli Politician, Israeli Prime Minister (2001–2006)

Benjamin Netanyahu — Statesman Of Israel. Israeli Prime Minister (1996–1999), Acting Prime Minister (From 2009)

Jean ChrEtien — Canadian Politician, 20Th Prime Minister Of Canada, Minister Of Justice Of Canada, Head Of Liberan Party Of Canada

Rudolph Giuliani — American Political Actor, Mayor Of New York Served From 1994 To 2001. Actor Of Republican Party

Colin Powell — Is An American Statesman And A Retired Four-Star General In The Us Army, 65Th United States Secretary Of State

Peter J. Daniels —
Is A Well-Known And
Respected Australian
Christian International
Business Statesman Of
Substance

Madeleine
Korbel Albright —
An American Politician And
Diplomat, 64Th United States
Secretary Of State

Kenneth Robert
Livingstone —
An English Politician,
1St Mayor Of London
(4 May 2000 – 4 May
2008), Labour Party
Representative

Sir Richard Charles Nicholas Branson —
English Business Magnate, Investor And Philanthropist. He Founded The *Virgin Group*, Which Controls More Than 400 Companies

Mel Gibson —
American Actor And Filmmaker

Chuck Norris —
American Martial Artist, Actor, Film Producer And Screenwriter

Christopher Tucker — American Actor And Comedian

Bernice Albertine King — American Minister Best Known As The Youngest Child Of Civil Rights Leaders Martin Luther King Jr. And Coretta Scott King Andrew

Andrew Young — American Politician, Diplomat, And Activist, 14[Th] United States Ambassador To The United Nations, 55[Th] Mayor Of Atlanta

General Wesley Kanne Clark — 4-Star General And Nato Supreme Allied Commander

Dr. Sunday Adelaja's family:
Perez, Pearl, Zoe and Pastor Bose Adelaja

FOLLOW SUNDAY ADELAJA ON SOCIAL MEDIA

Subscribe And Read Pastor Sunday's Blog:
www.sundayadelajablog.com
Follow these links and listen to over 200 of Pastor Sunday's Messages free of charge:
http://sundayadelajablog.com/content/
Follow Pastor Sunday on Twitter:
www.twitter.com/official_pastor

Join Pastor Sunday's Facebook page to stay in touch:
www.facebook.com/pastor.sunday.adelaja
Visit our websites for more information about Pastor Sunday's ministry:
http://www.godembassy.com
http://www.pastorsunday.com
http://sundayadelaja.de

CONTACT

FOR DISTRIBUTION OR TO ORDER
BULK COPIES OF THIS BOOK,
PLEASE CONTACT US:

USA
CORNERSTONE PUBLISHING
info@thecornerstonepublishers.com
+1 (516) 547-4999
www.thecornerstonepublishers.com

AFRICA
SUNDAY ADELAJA MEDIA LTD.
E-mail: btawolana@hotmail.com
+2348187518530, +2348097721451, +2348034093699

LONDON, UK
PASTOR ABRAHAM GREAT
abrahamagreat@gmail.com
+447711399828, +441908538141

KIEV, UKRAINE
pa@godembassy.org
Mobile: +380674401958

Best Selling Books by Dr. Sunday Adelaja
Available on Amazon.com and Okadabooks.com

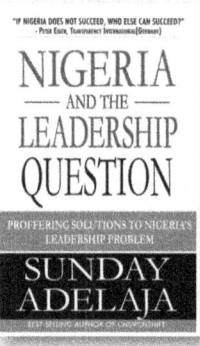

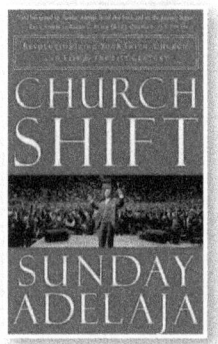
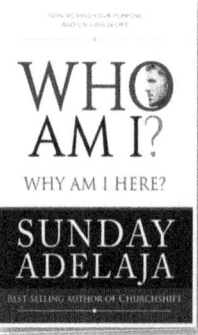

Best Selling Books by Dr. Sunday Adelaja
Available on Amazon.com and Okadabooks.com

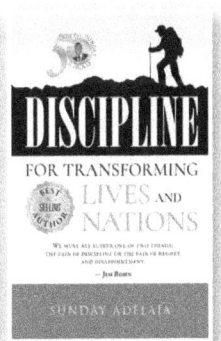
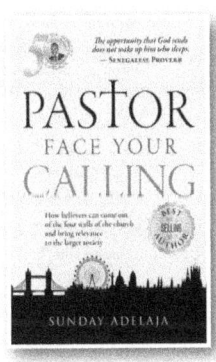

GOLDEN JUBILEE SERIES BOOKS
BY DR. SUNDAY ADELAJA

1. Who Am I
2. Only God Can Save Nigeria
3. The Mountain Of Ignorance
4. Stop Working For Uncle Sam
5. Poverty Mindset Vs Abundance Mindset
6. Raising The Next Generation Of Steve Jobs And Bill Gates
7. How To Build A Secured Financial Future
8. How To Become Great Through Time Conversion
9. Create Your Own Net Worth
10. Why You Must Urgently Become A Workaholic
11. How To Regain Your Lost Years
12. Pastor, Face Your Calling
13. Discipline For Transforming Lives And Nations
14. Excellence Your Key To Elevation
15. No One Is Better Than You
16. Problems Your Shortcut To Prominence
17. Let Heroes Arise!
18. How To Live An Effective Life
19. How To Win In Life
20. The Creative And Innovative Power Of A Genius
21. The Veritable Source Of Energy
22. The Nigerian Economy. The Way Forward
23. How To Get What You Need In Life
24. 7 Tips To Self-Fulfillment
25. Life Is An Opportunity
26. The Essence And Value Of Life
27. A Visionless Life Is A Meaningless Life
28. Where There Is Problem There Is Money
29. Work Is Better Than Vacation, Labour Better Than Favour
30. How To Overcome The Fear Of Death
31. Discovering The Purpose And Calling Of Nations
32. How To Become A Developed Nation Throught The Dignity Of Labor
33. Your Greatnes Is Proportional
34. Why Losing Your Job Is The Best Thing That Could Happen To You
35. What Do You Do With Your Time
36. Life Is Predictable
37. How To Be In The Here And Now
38. I Am A Person. Am I A Personality?
39. Discover The Source Of Your Latent Energy
40. How To Form Value Systems In A Child
41. Why I Am Unlucky
42. Hello! I Am Searching For Problems
43. Holistic Personality
44. How To transform And Build a Civilized Nation
45. Could You Be The Abraham Of Your Nation
46. The teambuilding skills of Jesus
47. How to keep your focus
48. The sin of irresponsibility
49. How Africans Brought Civilization To Europe
50. The Danger Of Monoculturalism

FOR DISTRIBUTION OR TO ORDER BULK COPIES OF THIS BOOKS, PLEASE CONTACT US:

USA | CORNERSTONE PUBLISHING
E-mail: info@thecornerstonepublishers.com, +1 (516) 547-4999
www.thecornerstonepublishers.com

AFRICA | SUNDAY ADELAJA MEDIA LTD.
E-mail: btawolana@hotmail.com
+2348187518530, +2348097721451, +2348034093699

LONDON, UK | PASTOR ABRAHAM GREAT
E-mail: abrahamagreat@gmail.com, +447711399828, +441908538141

KIEV, UKRAINE |
E-mail: pa@godembassy.org, Mobile: +380674401958

www.ingramcontent.com/pod-product-compliance
Lightning Source LLC
Chambersburg PA
CBHW031952080426
42735CB00007B/369